Do Children Drop Out of School in Kindergarten?

A Reflective, Systems-Based Approach for Promoting Deep Change

Do Children Drop Out of School in Kindergarten?

A Reflective, Systems-Based Approach for Promoting Deep Change

Gregory P. Hickman and Randy S. Heinrich

ROWMAN & LITTLEFIELD EDUCATION

A division of

ROWMAN & LITTLEFIELD PUBLISHERS, INC.
Lanham • New York • Toronto • Plymouth, UK

KH

Published by Rowman & Littlefield Education
A division of Rowman & Littlefield Publishers, Inc.
A wholly owned subsidiary of The Rowman & Littlefield Publishing Group, Inc.
4501 Forbes Boulevard, Suite 200, Lanham, Maryland 20706
http://www.rowmaneducation.com

Estover Road, Plymouth PL6 7PY, United Kingdom

Copyright © 2011 by Gregory P. Hickman and Randy S. Heinrich

British Library Cataloguing in Publication Information Available

Library of Congress Cataloging-in-Publication Data

Hickman, Gregory P., 1965–
  Do children drop out of school in kindergarten? : a reflective, systems-based approach for promoting deep change / Gregory P. Hickman and Randy S. Heinrich.
    p. cm.
  ISBN 978-1-61048-575-3 (cloth : alk. paper)—ISBN 978-1-61048-576-0 (pbk. : alk. paper)—ISBN 978-1-61048-577-7 (electronic)
  1. Dropouts—United States. 2. Dropouts—United States—Prevention. I. Heinrich, Randy S., 1959–. II. Title.
  LC143.H53 2011
  371.2'9130973—dc23
                                                                            2011025885

∞ ™ The paper used in this publication meets the minimum requirements of American National Standard for Information Sciences—Permanence of Paper for Printed Library Materials, ANSI/NISO Z39.48-1992.

Printed in the United States of America

11/26/12

Contents

Acknowledgments

We would like to express our sincere gratitude to Doctors Lattie Coor and Sybil Francis of the Center for the Future of Arizona (CFA). The study that offers the basis for this book was first conceptualized while the author Greg Hickman was the director of the Arizona Dropout Initiative at CFA. Without their gracious support and vision, this study would not have been feasible. We also would like to express our deep appreciation to Dr. Carol Peck of the Rodel Charitable Foundation. The author Greg Hickman, as director of the Rodel Community Scholars, was able to continue this study with co-author Randy Heinrich, as director of special services, Round Valley Schools (RVS), with support from the Rodel Charitable Foundation.

In addition, we thank Travis Udall, superintendent, and the wonderful staff at RVS for giving us access to student records to conduct this landmark study, and furnishing the lived experiences that deeply informed and inspired our view of school and community life in practical and potential terms for students and their families. We thank the Apache County Juvenile Probation Department for granting us access to their records to complement our findings. We thank Mitchell Bartholomew and Jennifer Mathwig for their efforts in writing the original publication of this study. We are indebted to Linda Swain for her editing support to improve the readability of our book and Dwight Getting for his patient, extensive help with producing the artwork. We deeply value the insights from a host of readers who took the time to review our draft book, including Karalea Cox, Susan Myers, Greg and Kathy Stopka, Amy Levinton, Travis Udall, Eleanor Pierce, Dr. Vanessa Girard, Dr. Marilyn Simon, Dr. Christine Ybarra, Bert Honigman, Scott Pochè, and Justin DeMello. Finally, we would like to thank our families, especially our wives Tammy and Donna, for their enduring support to our commitment to this very important endeavor.

Prologue

With the onset of successive iterations of the Elementary and Secondary Act (e.g., No Child Left Behind [NCLB]), educators, parents, and even the media have become focused on the recent events that surround the landmark legislation. Along with heightened requirements for today's education system comes the possibility for increased failure. For example, each year more state legislators are moving toward high school exit exams in an effort to meet NCLB requirements. As more state boards of education require exit exams for graduation, the probability of children dropping out of school increases. Because of such actions by state leaders, a major thrust of research and attention has been on high school dropouts.

A litany of research examines graduation and dropout rates. Further, numerous studies examine the relationship between a number of variables contributing to such rates and even the predictive nature and modeling of what creates a high school graduate and dropout. However, very little, if any, research has examined the longitudinal developmental pathways of graduates and dropouts from kindergarten to graduation or to the point of dropping out. Moreover, little, if any, research has thoroughly examined a child's entire academic, family, and behavioral past at each grade level during the child's time in school.

This book allows educators, parents, community stakeholders, political leaders, and students themselves to examine the complete developmental pathways of graduates and dropouts starting in kindergarten. More specifically, this book will highlight the complete academic, family, and behavioral variables at each grade level as they relate to graduates and dropouts. We will also make statistical comparisons between graduates and dropouts at each grade level. This approach will both help the reader examine student progress and allow educators, parents, therapists, intervention program staff evaluators, and other service professionals to establish interventions at key developmental periods.

In this book, we discuss our landmark research about dropouts and discuss the implications of the five major findings of our research:

Kindergarten—Dropouts and graduates appear very differently as they enter school and they follow distinct developmental pathways leading toward school failures and successes.

Absenteeism—Compared to graduates, dropouts spend much more time out of school from kindergarten onward.

Middle school (7th & 8th Grades)—Academic performance and absenteeism rates of dropouts and graduates differ noticeably during this period.

Ninth grade core courses—Dropouts take more core courses than graduates during the freshman year of high school and dropouts repeatedly struggle with core academic concepts.

Standardized test scores and academic performance—Dropouts perform better on standardized tests than they do in class, and the gap between dropouts' standardized test scores and classroom performance increases over time; graduates' standardized test scores and classroom performance remain relatively consistent over time.

This book offers powerful tools for engaging in deep change. We have structured the book by offering a brief overview of "what we know" regarding the "usual suspects" as they relate to dropouts in Chapter 1, "The Usual Suspects: What Do We Know Regarding Why Children Drop Out of School?" In Chapter 2, "Methodology," we provide an explanation of the methodology behind this study. In Chapter 3, "Background and Demographics," we provide background and demographic information so the reader can better understand the different backgrounds of dropouts and graduates when they start kindergarten. In Chapters 4 ("Does the Pathway to Dropping Out of School Really Start in Kindergarten?") through 8 ("Standardized Tests vs. Classroom Performance"), we provide details from our research regarding the topics of each of our five major findings. In Chapter 9, "Are Educational Pathways Set in Stone from Kindergarten?" we explore the possibility of whether those children who start out on the developmental pathway of dropping out of school in kindergarten can change their developmental pathway and graduate high school. Finally, in Chapter 10, "Understanding the Human Ecology: A Systems Approach in Understanding Why Children Drop Out of School," we close by discussing the importance of incorporating the human ecology of multiple systems to truly understand why students drop out of high school. Further, in Chapter 10, we provide a section entitled "What Works." In this section we discuss the five major findings of our study as related to dropout prevention from a systems perspective. We provide systems-based examples illustrating how to use action research principles to address the problems discussed in the preceding chapters.

The purpose of this book is to provide a glimpse into the developmental nature of high school graduates and dropouts from kindergarten onward and across all academic, family, and behavior variables.

For more information, please see www.dropouts101.com.

Chapter 1

The Usual Suspects

What Do We Know Regarding Why Children Drop Out of School?

The short answer to the question posed in the title of this book, *Do Children Drop Out of School in Kindergarten?*, is *yes*. When we peg youth as "problem children," carefully note their academic and social issues, count the numbers of mounting absences, offer remediation repeatedly (often at the expense of what may make learning joyful), and lower expectations about potential, should we be surprised that our children develop a sense of failure, low self-efficacy, disenfranchisement, and a desire to give up and drop out?

Currently, research regarding high school dropouts has centered on the identification and intervention of "at-risk" students with a propensity to drop out of school. Educational and community leaders, as well as policymakers, have incorporated available research and crafted numerous intervention programs and strategies targeted toward this audience. Unfortunately, many of these efforts have failed to demonstrate effectiveness—dropout rates across schools, districts, and states have remained the same.

The inability of educators, researchers, and program designers to effectively reduce the number of students dropping out of school may be grounded in their approach to understanding dropouts. More specifically, the driving force of research and dropout intervention programs has been tailored toward secondary education. Such a practice assumes an "educational vacuum" in a student's life from kindergarten to 8th grade. By ignoring the early years, educators and researchers may be overlooking the human ecology of students prior to the start of high school. In reality, adolescents experience many factors outside the education system that influence their development. Research regarding high school dropouts tends to use designs aimed at understanding linear relationships between specific variables, comparing variables that identify differences between dropouts and graduates, and predicting which

1

variables are related to dropouts. Such cause-and-effect thinking does not address the complexities that arise in the lives of youth in school, family, and community systems. As noted by the National Dropout Prevention Center, one of the greatest challenges in educational research is documenting long-term outcomes of early childhood educational experiences, a critical portion of the education system.

So the question we must ask is why educators and researchers continue to focus their efforts at the secondary level of education regarding high school dropouts when it seems inherent that the genesis of academic failure appears earlier in the student's educational development. In other words, evidence suggests student academic outcomes in high school are built upon the educational foundations developed prior to high school and are, furthermore, affected by education, family, and community systems. Still, there are indicators, or the "usual suspects," that drive dropout prevention efforts.

THE USUAL SUSPECTS

Academic Suspects

Educators have established that the child's shift from home life to school is an important transition. Making a successful shift from being at home to school is crucial in helping the child create an academic identity. Schools tend to operate in self-centered ways, doing business as if everyone lives on a bell schedule. Even as the child possesses different capabilities resulting from genetics, school, community, and home life, the American schooling process typically relies on traditional Socratic and eighteenth-century hierarchical models using mechanized processes with many prepackaged developmental expectations and interventions—useful for sorting types of students but with long-term implications for subsequent student self-regard.

Indicators that a student will eventually drop out of high school tend to appear within the first year of a child's schooling. The question becomes, when does the pathway between graduates and dropouts begin to look markedly different? Given the dissimilar experiences children encounter during their first five years of life, it is probable that not all children enter kindergarten with the developmental strengths required for subsequent academic success. The reading level at 3rd grade has been found across various studies to be a strong predictor of students who drop out of high school. Hence, 3rd grade has received notable attention as a possible "critical period" for increasing the chances of schooling success. It is thought that if actions are not taken by 3rd grade to correct academic deficits, particularly literacy preparation, those students who struggle will start on a downward academic spiral that may eventually lead to dropping out of school.

Perhaps the struggling student's noticeable literacy deficits in 3rd grade are a result of missing school. Research clearly demonstrates that attendance in kindergarten is highly predictive of attendance at higher levels of education. For example, a recent study of absenteeism found that dropouts averaged 16 days of absenteeism in kindergarten compared to 10 days of absenteeism for graduates. This six-day difference in absenteeism increased the likelihood of dropping out by 30%. Indeed, absenteeism in kindergarten has been linked to students' future academic attachment, identity, and success orientation.

Renowned psychologist Erik Erikson noted that a child must eventually go beyond taking initiative in the classroom. Rather, a child must learn to master academics, language, and social interactions. The lack of academic and social mastery appears to contribute to low self-regard about being able to successfully complete schoolwork. Low academic self-regard, along with poor attendance and grades, may eventually place a child on the pathway to dropping out of school. Perhaps the lack of academic mastery and success leads a child to feel as if he or she does not belong in school. The more a student feels he or she does not belong in school, the more school may become uninviting and unrewarding. Researchers have found that the earlier a child experiences academic failure and finds school uninviting and unrewarding, the less likely he/she will be to become successful and engaged later in school.

In an effort to combat the low academic self-regard that accompanies the lack of academic mastery and success, educators often retain or hold back a student to repeat a grade. One rationale for grade retention is that a child's deficits can be corrected. This approach suggests that the struggling student needs to adapt to the schooling process to perform in appropriate ways. It does not consider the possibility that the school staff might need to adapt instruction to help the struggling student learn in personally relevant ways. Nonetheless, an increasing body of research indicates that retention may not be the best answer and prove to be detrimental for student success in school. Further, retention tends to extend preexisting academic failure because students usually receive similar instruction that was not initially successful. When students are retained in the later elementary grades and middle school grades, they are at greater risk for future academic failure, including dropping out of school. Moreover, students who have experienced academic gains in early elementary grades while being held back tend to experience a "washout effect" several years later. In a ten-year longitudinal study of a large mentoring program, Greg Hickman, the co-author of this book, found that students held back in elementary school usually earned lower grades, experienced more disciplinary problems, performed below grade level, scored lower on standardized tests throughout their school careers, and dropped out of school more often than those students who were not retained.

Problem Behavior Suspects

Research clearly shows that adolescents who engage in problem behaviors are frequently identified early by teachers, parents, community leaders, peers, and therapists as potential dropouts. Further, research establishes relationships between a host of youth problem behaviors (such as underage drinking, drug abuse, family problems, probation, and incarceration) and school disciplinary and academic problems.

Although dropouts tend to experience heightened levels of disciplinary problems in schools, such behaviors appear to have origins outside the classroom. In a landmark study, Gerald Patterson, Barbara DeBaryshe, and Elizabeth Ramsey found that the antisocial progression of problem behavior stemmed from poor parental disciplining during the first five years of life. Upon entering kindergarten, children reared by parents who are ineffective at disciplining begin to exhibit conduct disorder behavioral problems. Children who exhibit conduct disorder behavioral problems are rejected by their peers and, consequently, develop a detachment from school because they find school academically and socially unrewarding.

During early adolescence, rejected children begin to congregate with each other for support, forming delinquent peer groups. While most children do not develop antisocial disorders, the parallel of related issues appears evident for struggling children who may come from homes of parents who are less effective than others in disciplining their children. Finally, as this developmental progression unfolds, adolescents may develop tendencies to drop out of high school.

As youth problem behaviors emerge across social settings, school and community members experience mixed results in trying to "help" these youth. Concerns about consequences and safety are often pitted against mercy and freedom to learn from mistakes. While traditionalists promote "tried and true" disciplinary methods that work well for many youth, non-traditionalists center discipline around an at-risk adolescent's experiences, sometimes leading to success. Still, research has strongly linked family characteristics with subsequent schooling challenges.

Family Suspects

Without a doubt, the family influences a child's academic, social, and emotional development. A recent study conducted by the Educational Policy

Studies Laboratory at Arizona State University surveyed parents across the state, asking, "What do you think is the single biggest reason why high school students drop out of school before finishing their education?" Thirty percent indicated that "home background" and "lack of parental involvement" were primary reasons students drop out of high school, with "family environment" being the most common response. Moreover, 82% of parental responses indicated psychological and social factors as reasons for dropping out of high school, while only 18% of parental responses found educational and school-related variables as reasons for children dropping out of high school.

A myriad of family factors are linked to high school dropouts. For example, students who have older siblings that drop out of high school tend to drop out at higher rates than students who do not have older siblings that drop out of high school. Students who come from lower socioeconomic status (SES) families tend to experience higher dropout rates than students who come from higher SES families. For example, Western Interstate Commission for Higher Education found the national high school graduation rate was 79.19% for students from families who exceed $100,000 per-year income, 77.06% for $50,000–$100,000 per-year income, 74.75% for $20,000–$49,999.99 per-year income, and 72.49% for students from families that earn below $20,000 per-year income.

Family mobility has also been found to play a role in the academic development of children. Families who move around a lot have children who experience greater difficulties adjusting academically, socially, and emotionally to new schools. Further, students who experience many moves appear to be less attached and engaged in school than their counterparts who do not experience many moves during school. Despite the litany of research confirming that a child's family is essential to academic success, educators and researchers struggle to connect family and school when addressing children's educational needs.

Given these "usual suspects" (i.e., academic, behavioral, community, and family variables) and dropout prevention research studies that typically focus on comparing variables using cause-and-effect or comparison reasoning to understand high school dropouts, we decided to conduct a long-term study of the developmental pathways of dropouts and graduates at each grade level during their school careers across academic subjects/courses, grades, standardized tests, family factors, language, behavior, and county juvenile court information. Consequently, this study advanced what we know regarding high school dropouts by essentially contrasting dropouts' and graduates' entire academic, family, behavioral history as listed in school, and, in some cases, juvenile records.

Chapter 2

Methodology

Without a doubt, successive legislative initiatives of the Elementary and Secondary Education Act (e.g., No Child Left Behind) have generated a vast amount of research and inquiry regarding high school dropouts and the methods for measuring dropout rates. Although researchers and educators differ in the method of defining who is a dropout and calculating dropout rates, they are in agreement that approximately every nine seconds a student decides to permanently leave high school prior to graduation; in other words, one in four students in America leaves school before graduating. Such a premature departure from school has prompted policymakers to address the steep educational, economic, and civic effects of dropouts on society.

Do Children Drop Out of School in Kindergarten? is based on two research questions from our study. First, do differences exist in the developmental pathways of high school graduates and high school dropouts? Second, if differences do exist in the developmental pathways of high school graduates and high school dropouts, when and where do these differences occur?

PARTICIPANTS

Official school data were obtained by randomly choosing 119 school records from four school year groups (2002–2005) from a school district in east central Arizona. Sixty graduating students and sixty dropouts were randomly chosen from the 2002–2005 school groups. One dropout student was dismissed from the study because there were no data in the chosen academic file. Females comprised 49.2% of the sample, males 50.8%. The ethnic representation included Caucasian American (77.8%), Hispanic (15.7%), and Native American (6.5%)

students, a ratio similar to school and Arizona state populations. While 60 students graduated from high school, 59 students dropped out of school between their sophomore and junior years (average = 10.58th grade). Average family income for families living within the school district area was $29,500.00.

PROCEDURES

Participants in this study were students enrolled in the 2002–2005 cohorts. (A *cohort* is a group of students who started kindergarten in a given year and were tracked over time to the point of graduating or dropping out of high school.) Students from these cohorts started kindergarten in the years 1990–1993. After the sampling procedure was completed, we examined the contents of the students' school files. Each file contained report cards; progress reports; letters to parents; attendance records; disciplinary infractions; family background variables such as family size, siblings, and parental occupation; standardized tests scores; high school transcripts; earned credit hours; and the graduation or dropout date. In addition, official county juvenile court records were obtained for those students in the sample who received such services.

To remain consistent, we examined student subject (elementary years) and course (middle school and high school years) performance grades of core subjects and courses from kindergarten through 12th grade or to the point of dropout. For kindergarten through 8th grade, we examined students' course performance grades in writing, English, mathematics, reading, spelling, social studies, and science. For 9th grade through 12th grade, we looked at students' core course performance grades in English and mathematics because they tend to be the primary indicators of academic success. In addition, these core courses comprised two of the three components of the state high school exit exam. Secondary analysis performance grades of core courses such as sciences and social studies were also examined during 9th grade to gain an understanding of each student's academic background prior to entering high school.

Subject and course performance evaluations varied across grades. For example, all subject grades in kindergarten were recorded as *satisfactory*, *needs improvement*, or *unsatisfactory*. We assigned the following numeric values: "satisfactory" = 0, "needs improvement" = 1, and "unsatisfactory" = 2. We coded satisfactory as zero so we could see any scores above zero as deviating from satisfactory. Hence, the higher the score indicated in our study the less satisfactory the grade. The majority of students' subject performance grades in 1st through 2nd grades were similarly recorded. However, some students' subject performance grades in 1st through 2nd grades were recorded in Arabic scale (i.e., A, A–, B+, B, B–, C+, C, C–, D, D+, D–, and F). These grades were then re-coded into the grade point value (i.e., A = 4.0, A– = 3.7, B+ = 3.3, B = 3.0, B– = 2.7, C+ = 2.3, C = 2.0, C– = 1.7, D+ = 1.3, D = 1.0, D– = .7, and F = 0.0) used by the school district and converted to a grade point average (GPA). All students' subject and course performance grades in 3rd through 12th grades were initially recorded in Arabic scale, so we just had to convert them to a GPA. Subject and course performance grades were taken from official report cards and transcripts.

MEASURES

Variables were measured and obtained via official school and county juvenile court records. Variables included (a) specific subject and course grades; (b) GPA; (c) core classes; (d) proficiency test scores; (e) grade retention; (f) absenteeism; (g) family and demographic variables; and (h) county juvenile court records.

Specific Subject and Course Grades/GPA. Please see Table 2.1 for an example of how specific subject and/or course grades were re-coded based on report cards and/or transcripts.

9th Grade Total Core Courses. We decided which courses would be considered primary academic indicators and which would be considered secondary academic indicators. For example, if a student's transcript indicated that the student took English, mathematics, science, art, physical education, band, and history during his or her freshman year and the school district administration considered English, mathematics, science, and history to be core courses, then he or she received credit for four core classes. The school district in this study did not consider art, physical education, and band core courses, so these courses were not addressed in our study.

Stanford Achievement Tests. Stanford Achievement Tests (SATs) have demonstrated reliability and validity, and they are used for evaluative purposes by college, university, and government agency staffs. SATs, given to students in 1st–9th grades, are designed to measure achievement in word-study skills,

Table 2.1. Grade Conversion

Course	Credit	Letter Grade	Numeric Grade Value
Math	1.0	B+	3.3
English	1.0	C	2.0
Science	1.0	A–	3.7
History	1.0	C+	2.3
Art	0.5	A	4.0
Physical Education	0.5	A	4.0
Band	0.5	A	4.0

reading comprehension, vocabulary, listening comprehension, spelling, language, number concepts, mathematical applications and computations, and social sciences. Total subject scores range from 1 to 99, with an average or National Curve Equivalency (NCE) of 50.

Total NCE reading, math, and language scores were derived from student records and selected for analysis because these scores tend to be predictors of academic success. Because students transfer in and out of various schools, many standardized tests scores are not transferred to a student's file when they move from one school to another school. Consequently, not enough data from Stanford scores in 1st–4th grades were available. Hence, only SAT scores between 5th and 9th grades were used in this study.

Grade Retention. Grade retention was measured by examining official school records of a student's lack of advancement to the next grade level and was coded as "retained" = 0 and "not retained" = 1. School records were recorded yearly as to what grade level the student completed and the grade the student was enrolled in every given year over the student's school history. Examining such records, we were able to detect at what grade, if any, and how many times a student was retained in K–8th grade.

Absenteeism. Absenteeism was measured by examining official school records of the days a student missed school at each grade level from K–8th grade. Absenteeism was based on ¼, ½, ¾, and 1 full day missed from school. Days absent were recorded regardless of whether it was an excused absence or not.

Family and Demographics. Several family and personal variables were examined from official student records. Because there are a number of family arrangements, students were characterized as coming from either a two-parent home = 0 or other family structure = 1. Student birth certificates were used to determine birth location and to sort students by who was "Arizona born" = 0, and "non-Arizona born" = 1. Family sibling information included the number of a participant's siblings and number of siblings that were older than the participant. Ethnicity was separated into "Caucasian" = 0 and "non-Caucasian" = 1. Gender was coded as "male" = 0 and "female" = 1. Of those who were qualified, free and/or reduced lunch (FRL) and Title I services participants were coded as "yes" = 0 and non-participants were coded as "no" = 1. All family variables were obtained from official school records.

County Juvenile Court Records. A list of study participants was provided to the county juvenile court. The court then provided records for adjudicated youth involved in the study, regardless of their graduation status. The court annotated age, date adjudicated, and type of sentence (i.e., diversion program, standard and/or intense probation, and incarceration). The data were coded as "not adjudicated" = 0 and "yes adjudicated" = 1.

Statistical Analyses

Because the numbers of students and study-related variables differed across grade levels and, in some cases, in the school files, whenever the sample size was less than 30, we used statistical analysis that compared variables to see trends. When the sample size exceeded 30, we used statistical testing that could determine probabilities of recurrences of the findings in similar settings. For the probability testing, we compared graduates and dropouts against specific course grades, GPAs, proficiency test scores, grade retention, family variables, absenteeism, core classes taken freshman year, and county juvenile court records across all grades (K–12) or to the point of dropout.

For purposes of this book only, descriptive mean comparisons between graduates and dropouts will be addressed across all variables of study as opposed to inferential probability testing typically conducted in scientific journals, as such statistical procedures go beyond the scope of this book. However, for those interested in the probability findings, please refer to our study in the *Journal of Educational Research* published in 2008. Bottom line, please understand that the differential findings between graduates and dropouts in this study were significant as early as kindergarten.

In summary, the research method used for *Do Children Drop Out of School in Kindergarten?* provides strong evidence regarding the nature of the differential developmental pathways followed by high school graduates and dropouts across each grade level and across all variables recorded in their school history. Basically, we believe that, at some point early in their developmental pathways, those students who drop out of high school begin to look markedly different from their peers who graduate from high school.

Chapter 3

Background and Demographics

This study took place in a school district located in the White Mountains region of Arizona. Located northeast of Phoenix, Arizona, the school district enrolls children who reside in two communities and surrounding areas with a combined population of approximately 9,000 citizens and a combined land mass of approximately 23 square miles. Like many rural communities in Arizona and across the United States, families residing in the White Mountains rely on tourism, agriculture, construction, forest service, hunting, fishing, lumbering, cattle and sheep ranching, power plant operations, hospitality industries, and retail sales as their major sources of employment and economy.

GENDER AND ETHNIC DEMOGRAPHICS

As mentioned in Chapter 2, statistical analyses presented in text, tables, and figures presented in this chapter are based on the 119 students (60 graduates and 59 dropouts) of our sample. The ethnic distribution of the study's participants included Caucasian (77.8%), Hispanic (15.7%), and Native American (6.5%) students, a distribution similar to school and state demographics. (See Figure 3.1 for a graphical view of ethnic data.)

Graduates in this study were more likely to be Caucasian (65%) than Native American and Hispanic collectively (30.2%). Graduation rates of the Caucasian students in this study were slightly lower than the state Caucasian graduation rate of approximately 72% and the national Caucasian graduation rate of approximately 77%. During the period of this study, graduation rates for Hispanic and Native American students collectively in this study were lower than the state and national graduation rates of approximately 50% for Hispanic and Native American students.

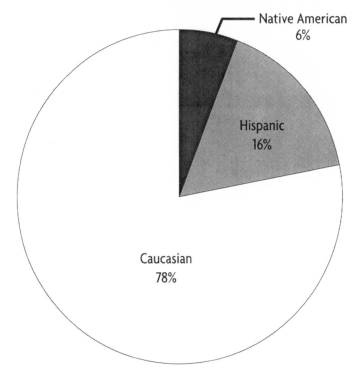

Figure 3.1. Ethnic Background of Sample

FAMILY INCOME DEMOGRAPHICS

The median family income of this region is approximately $34,000 per year, which is slightly above the Arizona median family income of $29,500 per year and significantly below the national median family income of approximately $42,000 per year. The five most common occupations of students' fathers in our study were carpenters, loggers, laborers, machine operators, and welders while the five most common occupations of mothers were housewives, nurses, secretaries, bartenders, and laborers. This was consistent with occupations of males and females throughout the White Mountains region in Arizona.

With student-family income data not often available at local, district, and state education levels, educational comparisons of family income are difficult to obtain. As a result, educators have used FRL as a measure of obtaining family income and/or socioeconomic status (SES). To be eligible for FRL, a family's income must be below a certain financial cutoff, depending on the number of dependents in a household. Each school is designated a value ranging from zero to one hundred percent, based on the percentage of students who qualify for FRL. Hence, the higher the percentage a school is designated as FRL, the lower the family income is of those students enrolled in that school. In our study, a significant difference was found: 45.5% of graduates participated in the schools' FRL program while 60% of dropouts participated in the schools' FRL program. Hence, it appears that dropouts are coming from lower-income families with the need for school lunch assistance. See Table 3.1 for side-by-side comparisons of dropouts and graduates regarding FRL.

Another indicator of family income is Title I services received by students. According to Title I, all youth deserve a fair chance at achieving academic standards and school success. Title I services were usually furnished to former Head Start students (low income eligible), homeless students, and students who performed poorly on grade-level-appropriate literacy screening and test scores. In our study, dropouts comprised 69.2% and graduates comprised 30.8% of those students who received Title I services. As you can see, the "usual suspects" of poverty, poor academic readiness, and low family income, along with the stigmas of receiving FRL and/or Title I services at

Table 3.1. Side-by-Side Comparisons of the "Usual Suspects"

Usual Suspect	Graduates	Dropouts
Free and/or Reduced Lunch	45.50%	60.00%
Title I Services	30.80%	69.20%
Biological Intact Family	60.60%	39.10%
Large Family Size	44.30%	59.10%
Zero Siblings	30.80%	69.20%
One Sibling	78.80%	22.20%
Three or Fewer Older Siblings	55.10%	44.90%
Four or More Older Siblings	20.00%	80.00%
Born Outside Arizona	37.90%	62.10%
High Family Mobility (4+ Moves)	46.50%	53.50%
Credits	26.75%	7.28%
No Extracurricular Activities	28.00%	72.90%
English Language Learners	29.60%	71.40%
Grade of 1st Official School Disciplinary Record	6th grade	4th grade
School Disciplinary Actions	27.30%	72.70%

Juvenile Justice System	Graduates	Dropouts
Diversion Program–1 Time	36.40%	63.60%
Diversion Program–2 Times	28.60%	71.40%
Diversion Program–Age 15+	50.00%	50.00%
Diversion Program–Age 14	21.40%	78.60%
Probation	17.70%	82.30%
Probation–Age 15+	18.20%	81.80%
Probation–Age 14 below	16.70%	83.30%
Intense Probation	0.00%	100.00%

school, appear to have affected future dropouts more than future graduates. (See Table 3.1 for side-by-side comparisons of dropouts and graduates regarding Title I services.)

FAMILY BACKGROUND DEMOGRAPHICS

Family *structure* has received much attention by researchers as a "usual suspect" toward predicting academic and behavioral problems in children and adolescents. In our study, 67.6% of students came from biologically intact families where mom and dad were married and never divorced, whereas 32.4% of students came from divorced, single-mother, and other family structures. We found that 39.1% of students from biologically intact families dropped out of high school whereas 60.6% of students from divorced, single-mother, and other family structures dropped out of high school.

Family *size* has also received attention, albeit to a lesser extent, from educators as a "usual suspect" in predicting academic and behavioral problems in children and adolescents. According to the US Census, the national average family size is 3.14 persons per family. For this study, we considered any family size of five members or more to be a large family. Based on the students in our study, 78.2% came from families with four or fewer members, while 21.8% came from families with five or more members. Almost 60% (59.1%) of students who came from large families of five or more members dropped out of high school compared to 44.3% of students from smaller families. Once family size reached six or more members, 77.8% of students dropped out of high school.

The number of siblings in families has long been a predictor of academic and behavioral problems in children and adolescents. For example, research has demonstrated that being the only child or having older siblings leads to poor academic achievement, teenage pregnancy, lower educational achievement, and adjudication in the juvenile justice system. In our study, 69.2% of students without siblings dropped out of school while 30.8% of students without siblings graduated from school. However, only 22.2% of students with one sibling dropped out of school while 78.8% of students with one sibling graduated from school. In our study we found that as the family size increased, the percentage of students that dropped out also increased. Indeed, we found that 100% of students in our study who had five or more siblings dropped out of high school. Further, not one graduate in our study came from a family with five or more siblings.

The number of *older* siblings has also been a "usual suspect" in predicting academic and problematic behaviors. In our study we found that 44.9% of students with 3 or fewer older siblings dropped out of school while 55.1% of students with 3 or fewer older siblings graduated from school. However, 80% of students with 4 or more older siblings dropped out of school while only 20% of students with 4 or more older siblings graduated from school. Indeed, we found that 100% of students in our study with 5 or more older siblings dropped out of high school. Further, not one graduate in our study came from a family with 5 or more older siblings.

In addition to family income, family structure, family size, and age of siblings, family mobility has also been tagged as a "usual suspect" of predicting academic and behavioral problems of children and adolescents. The thought behind this assumption is that because children and adolescents are moving and experiencing multiple transitions in their lives, they do not form attachments to their communities, schools, and peers. In our study, 71.8% of students were born in Arizona while 28.2% of students were born outside of Arizona. Interestingly, 45.9% of those students born in the state of Arizona dropped out of high school, whereas 62.1% of those students born outside the state of Arizona dropped out of high school.

Given such differences in dropout by place of birth, we decided to examine family mobility. More specifically, we defined high family mobility as four or more transitional moves in and out of school districts. In our study, 73.8% of students had experienced fewer than four transitional moves or low family mobility, whereas 26.2% of students had experienced four or more transitional moves or high family mobility. As expected, 43% of those students experiencing low family mobility dropped out of school, whereas 53.5% of those students experiencing high family mobility dropped out of school. See Table 3.1 for side-by-side comparisons of dropouts and graduates regarding family background variables.

EDUCATIONAL BACKGROUND DEMOGRAPHICS

Out of 119 students in the study, 60 students graduated from high school, while 59 students dropped out of school between their sophomore and junior year (Mean = 10.58th grade). Dropouts received 7.28 high school credits compared to graduates' 26.75 high school credits. In our study, 44.2% of students enrolled in vocational courses, while 55.8% of students did not enroll in vocational courses. Of those students who enrolled in vocational courses, 52.1% dropped out of high school, whereas only 39.6% of those students that did not enroll in vocational courses dropped out of high school.

In our study, 17.3% of students qualified for special education services. The other 82.7% of students did not qualify for special education services. Sixty percent of those students who qualified for special education services dropped out of high school while only 49% of students that did not qualify for special education services dropped out of high school.

Finally, 57.5% of students were involved in extracurricular activities (i.e., band, music, choir, drama, intramural sports, and various clubs and school programs) at school while 42.5% of students were not involved. Of those students involved in extracurricular activities, only 28.0% dropped out of high school, whereas 72.9% of those students *not* involved in extracurricular activities dropped out of high school. Even more interesting is that not one dropout was involved in extracurricular activities at school prior to 6th grade while graduates were involved in extracurricular activities as early as kindergarten. Hence, extracurricular activity involvement at school was one of the biggest differences between dropouts and graduates in this study, supporting the notion that children involved in school stay in school.

It also appears that, taken together, education and family affect children at school. For example, the southwest region of the United States tends to experience a high percentage of family mobility because many Hispanic migrant workers continually move during the agricultural season to meet work needs. As a result, children from such families often change schools. Many of these migrant workers do not speak English; Spanish is the primary language spoken at home. As a result, such students tend to be designated at their schools as English Language Learners (ELL). In our study, 49.1% of non-ELL students dropped out of high school while 71.4% of ELL students dropped out of high school. See Table 3.1 for side-by-side comparisons of dropouts and graduates regarding educational background variables.

BEHAVIORAL BACKGROUND AND DEMOGRAPHICS

Without doubt, one of the best predictors or "usual suspects" of dropping out of high school is related to problem behaviors. Children and adolescents who experience school infractions, suspensions, and expulsions tend to struggle with academics compared to children and adolescents that do not engage in such behavioral problems. Research has clearly linked academic problems and failure at school to similar behaviors in the community as evidenced by offenses that render children and adolescents adjudicated, in some capacity, by the juvenile justice system. Furthermore, the earlier a child is identified by school officials as being problematic and adjudicated by the juvenile justice system, the more likely their poor prognosis for future academic and behavioral problems.

First, we set out to see if the students in our study had received "official" disciplinary action as indicated by school records in their academic files. It is interesting to note that almost half (48.2%) of students had *not* received any disciplinary actions while just over half (51.8%) of students *had* received some sort of disciplinary actions. Alarmingly, 72.7% of students that received disciplinary actions at some point in their school life dropped out of school while only 17.1% of students that had not received disciplinary actions dropped out of high school. Further, the average grade level of a dropout's first "official" disciplinary action was approximately 4th grade; graduates' average grade level at first infraction was 6th grade. This supports research indicating that the younger a child is identified as being a "problem," the less likely he or she will be to graduate high school.

Disciplinary infractions can result in school suspensions and, in extreme cases, even expulsions from school. In our study, students that dropped out of high school were suspended as early as 8th grade. Incredibly, not one student who was suspended graduated high school. No students in our study were expelled.

We also partnered with the County Juvenile Probation Department in an effort to determine if there were differences in involvement in diversion programs, standard probation, intense probation, and incarceration of those students who dropped out and graduated high school. We found that 45.2% of students not involved in juvenile diversion programs dropped out of school while 63.6% of students involved in juvenile diversion programs once and 71.4% of students involved twice dropped out of school. The average age of students who became involved in juvenile diversion programs was 14 years of age. Of those students involved in juvenile diversion programs at age 14 or younger, 78.6% dropped out of high school while 50% of those students involved in juvenile diversion programs at age 15 or older dropped out of high school. This supports research that the younger a child is entered into the juvenile justice system, the less likely it is he or she will graduate high school.

In addition to diversion programs we looked at students placed on probation from the juvenile justice system. In our study, only 14.6% of students were placed on probation; 85.4% of students were not placed on probation. We found that 45.0% of students not involved in juvenile probation dropped out of high school whereas 82.3% of students involved in juvenile probation dropped out of high school. The average age of students being placed on probation was 14.76 years of age. Of those students placed on juvenile probation at age 14 or younger, 83.3% dropped out of high school; a similar percentage of students placed on juvenile probation at age 15 or older (81.8%) also dropped out of high school. We also looked at intense probation. Although only 5.9% of the students in this study were on intense probation, all of them (100%) dropped out of high school. Finally, no students in the study were incarcerated in the juvenile justice system.

As can be seen from this study, the "usual suspects" of family structure, family size, family income, family mobility, FRL, Title I services, ELL services, special education services, vocational courses, extracurricular activities, disciplinary actions, school suspensions, involvement with the juvenile justice system, and age identified as being problematic are all supported in this study.

The question that remains elusive to educators and researchers is how do these "usual suspects" work or operate as a system in leading children to drop out of high school? These "usual suspects" were examined in a cause-and-effect, linear fashion—stated differently, each individual "usual suspect" (e.g., family, academic, behavioral) is related to children dropping out. What is lost in the mix is how different participants, perspectives, and ecologies all work together to lead a child down the developmental pathway of dropping out of high school. We will explore this in further detail in Chapter 10. We will recommend that only when educators and researchers consider the complexities of human ecology as it relates to school success will they begin to understand why children drop out of high school.

Now that the reader is familiar with the background and demographics of the students in this study, we will, over the course of the next five chapters, illustrate the five major findings of this study.

Chapter 4

Does the Pathway to Dropping Out of School Really Start in Kindergarten?

Before we examine the five major findings of this study, it is important to remind the reader of the two research questions postulated for this study. First, do differences exist in the developmental pathways of high school graduates compared to high school dropouts? Although we thought such differences did exist between graduates and dropouts, we had to use this question as our starting point. In a sense, the answer to this question gave us the license, so to speak, to move forward and ask the next question. Second, if differences do exist in the developmental pathways of high school graduates compared to high school dropouts, where in time and across which variables do these differences occur? And as mentioned in previous chapters, our study and our answers, as presented in the text, tables, and figures of this chapter, are based on the statistical analysis of the 119 students (60 graduates and 59 dropouts) of our sample.

WHAT WE FOUND

It should be noted up front that the persistent and clear developmental differences in pathways between graduates and dropouts that were unfolded in the findings of this study were shocking, to say the least. Although we thought differences would exist between graduates and dropouts, we certainly did not expect to see a recurrent theme and clear diverging pathways between graduates and dropouts that started in kindergarten.

K–12 Academic Subject/Course Evaluations

K–2 subject performance grades and 3–12 subject/course performance grades were reported in GPA form as addressed in Chapter 2.

K–2nd Grade Academic Course Performance. Qualitative performance differences between dropouts and graduates appeared to exist as early as kindergarten. For example, kindergarten reading performance grades for high school dropouts (Average = .60) was significantly lower than kindergarten reading for high school graduates (Average = .06). Kindergarten writing performance for high school dropouts (Average = .29) was significantly lower than kindergarten in writing performance for high school graduates (Average = .00). Kindergarten mathematics performance for high school dropouts (Average = .43) was significantly lower than kindergarten mathematics performance for high school graduates (Average = .06). Kindergarten spelling performance for high school dropouts (Average = .17) was lower than kindergarten spelling performance of high school graduates (Average = .00). Finally, kindergarten English performance for high school dropouts (Average = .33) was lower than kindergarten English performance for high school graduates (Average = .00). Indeed, almost every graduate achieved a "Satisfactory" performance grade across all core subjects while dropouts achieved "Needs Improvement" or "Unsatisfactory" as early as kindergarten. This developmental pattern continues while both graduates and dropouts are subject to qualitative performance grades across all subjects. Although not reported, the same developmental pattern holds true for non-core subjects such as music, art, choir, band, and physical education. See Table 4.1 for a complete summary.

1st–8th Grade Academic Subject/Course Performance. GPA performance differences between dropouts and graduates appeared to exist as early as 1st

Table 4.1. Course Performance Grades K–2 (Satisfactory = 0, Needs Improvement = 1, Unsatisfactory = 2)

Group	Kindergarten	1st Grade	2nd Grade
	Average Reading Performance		
Dropouts	0.60	0.25	0.20
Graduates	0.06	0.13	0.03
	Average Writing performance		
Dropouts	0.29	0.07	0.00
Graduates	0.00	0.03	0.00
	Average Math Performance		
Dropouts	0.43	0.00	0.08
Graduates	0.06	0.04	0.00
	Average Spelling Performance		
Dropouts	0.17	0.22	0.00
Graduates	0.00	0.04	0.06
	Average English Performance		
Dropouts	0.33	0.20	0.64
Graduates	0.00	0.09	0.03

grade in reading, spelling, English, writing, and mathematics subjects and courses, and as early as 2nd grade for science and social studies. For example, 1st grade reading performance for high school dropouts (Average = 2.66) was significantly lower than 1st grade reading performance for high school graduates (Average = 3.61). See Figure 4.1.

First grade mathematics performance for high school dropouts (Average = 2.67) was significantly lower than for high school graduates (Average = 3.49). See Figure 4.2.

First grade writing performance for high school dropouts (Average = 3.39) was significantly lower than for high school graduates (Average = 2.88). See Figure 4.3.

First grade English performance was significantly lower for dropouts (Average = 2.67) than for high school graduates (Average = 3.46). See Figure 4.4.

First grade spelling performance was significantly lower for high school dropouts (Average = 2.42) than for high school graduates (Average = 3.31). See Figure 4.5.

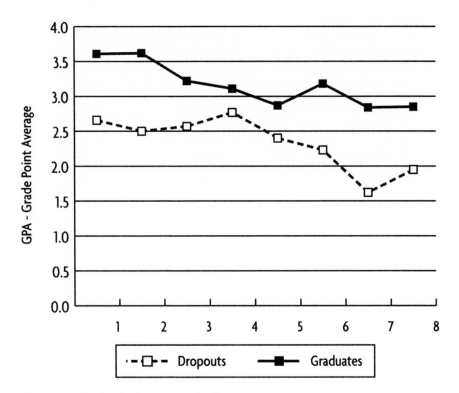

Figure 4.1. Reading Performance—Grades 1–8

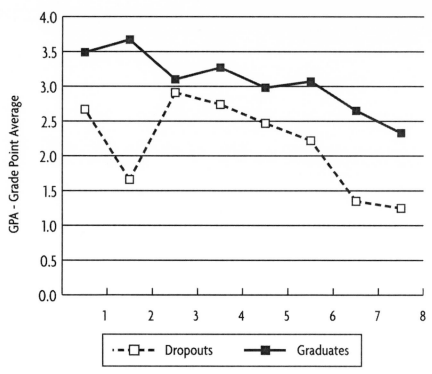

Figure 4.2. Math Performance—Grades 1–8 (G. P. Hickman, M. Bartholomew, J. Mathwig, and R. S. Heinrich [2008]. "Differential developmental pathways of high school dropouts and graduates," *Journal of Educational Research*, 102(1), 3–14. © Taylor & Francis Ltd, http://www.tandf.co.uk/journals, reprinted by permission of publisher.)

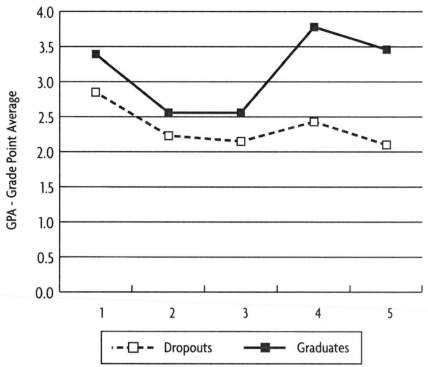

Figure 4.3. Writing Performance—Grades 1–5

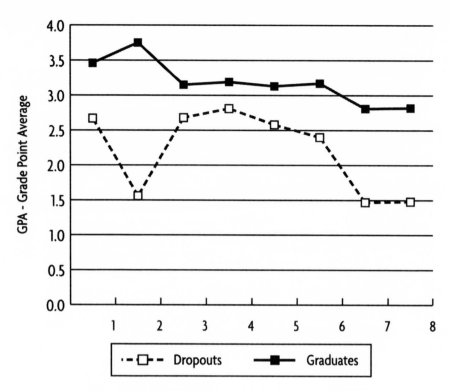

Figure 4.4. English Performance—Grades 1–8

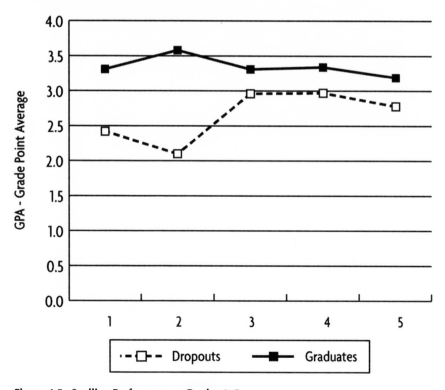

Figure 4.5. Spelling Performance—Grades 1–5

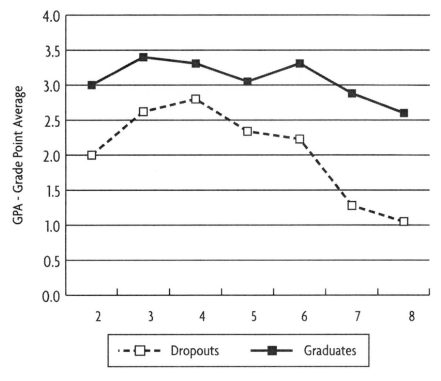

Figure 4.6. Social Studies Performance—Grades 2–8

Second grade social studies performance for high school dropouts (Average = 2.00) was significantly lower than 2nd grade social studies performance for high school graduates (Average = 3.00). Social studies was not recorded quantitatively at this school district until 2nd grade. Hence, at the earliest grade possible, dropouts and graduates differed in this subject. See Figure 4.6.

Second grade science performance was significantly lower for high school dropouts (Average = 2.50) than for high school graduates (Average = 4.00). Like social studies, science grades were not recorded quantitatively until 2nd grade. See Figure 4.7.

As can be seen in Figures 4.1–4.7, not only do differences between dropouts and graduates in the aforementioned subjects and courses begin early in life, but the differential gaps in the developmental pathways of both graduates and dropouts also widen and do not deviate from the start of their time in school.

9th–12th Grade Academic Course Performance. Overall GPA performance differences between high school dropouts and graduates were evident

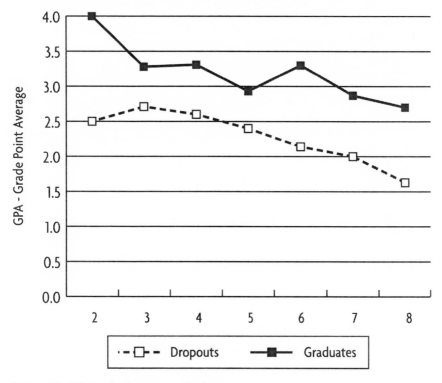

Figure 4.7. Science Performance—Grades 1–8

as early as the first semester of the 9th grade year. For example, 9th grade first semester overall GPA for high school dropouts (Average = 1.27) was significantly lower than 9th grade first semester overall GPA for high school graduates (Average = 2.75). These differences between dropouts and graduates remained significant in every semester and grade level throughout the tenure of a high school student. Indeed, regardless of whether a student graduated or dropped out of high school, the best predictor of the student's final high school GPA was his or her academic performance during the first semester of 9th grade. See Figure 4.8.

Because English and mathematics are two of the three components of the Arizona state exit exam at the time of our study, only these core subject courses will be discussed. Dropouts' English 1 performance (Average = 1.12) was significantly lower than graduates' English 1 performance (Average = 2.49). Clearly, high school graduates and dropouts remained on their developmental course—neither graduates nor dropouts deviated in their course performances as they progressed from English 1 to English 4. See Figure 4.9.

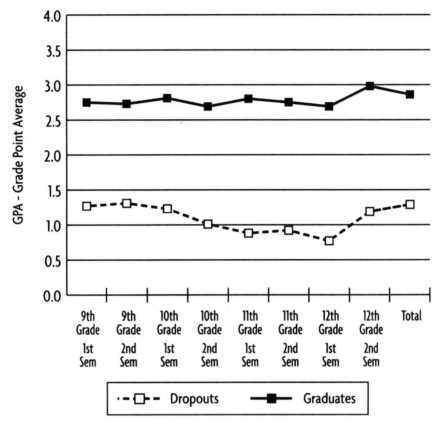

Figure 4.8. Academic Course Performance (GPA)—Grades 9–12

Further, dropouts took on average 1.6 English courses in high school whereas graduates took, on average, 4 high school English courses. Even more interesting is that dropouts achieved, on average, a .76 GPA on the highest English course they took whereas graduates achieved, on average, a 2.26 on the highest English course they took. See Figure 4.10.

Figure 4.11 demonstrates that dropouts and graduates differ significantly in the level of mathematical courses taken during high school and Figure 4.12 demonstrates the highest grade achieved in the highest mathematical course taken in high school. For example, dropouts' highest-level mathematical course completed was between pre-algebra and algebra, with the average being closer to pre-algebra. Conversely, graduates' highest mathematical course completed was between geometry and algebra, with the average being closer to geometry. Moreover, the average GPA (1.02 GPA) for dropouts in the highest math course

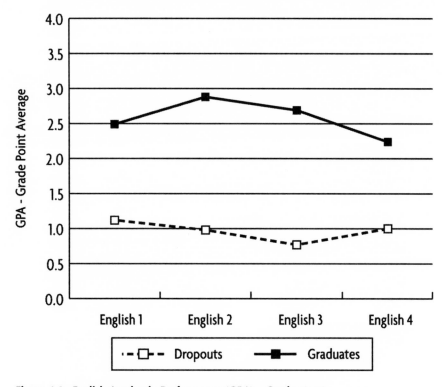

Figure 4.9. English Academic Performance (GPA)—Grades 9–12

(pre-algebra) they completed was significantly lower than the average GPA (2.04 GPA) in the highest math course (geometry) completed by graduates.

Stanford Achievement Tests. Differences were observed in Stanford testing scores in various 5th grade total NCE achievement scores between high school graduates and dropouts. For example, total NCE reading scores were significantly lower for high school dropouts (Average = 46.33) than for high school graduates (Average = 54.72). Not only did differences exist in 5th grade between high school graduates and dropouts, but the gap also widened as students progressed from 5th grade to 9th grade. Moreover, those students that graduated remained relatively steady in their reading scores from 5th to 9th grade while those students that dropped out decreased their reading scores from 5th to 9th grade. See Figure 4.13.

Fifth grade total NCE mathematical scores were significantly lower for high school dropouts (Average = 32.28) than for high school graduates (Average = 41.26). As with total NCE reading scores, not only did differences exist in 5th grade between high school graduates and dropouts, but

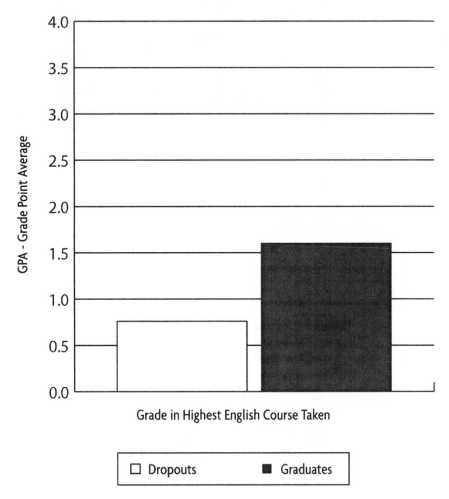

Figure 4.10. High School English Data

the gap widened as students progressed from 5th to 9th grade. Students that dropped out of school experienced smaller gains in their mathematical scores from 5th to 9th grade, whereas students that graduated experienced increased gains in their mathematical scores from 5th to 9th grade. See Figure 4.14.

Fifth grade total NCE language scores were significantly lower for high school dropouts (Average = 40.19) than for high school graduates (Average = 44.66). Not only did differences exist in 5th grade between high school graduates and dropouts, but the gap also widened as students progressed from 5th grade to 9th grade. Moreover, those students that graduated increased their language scores

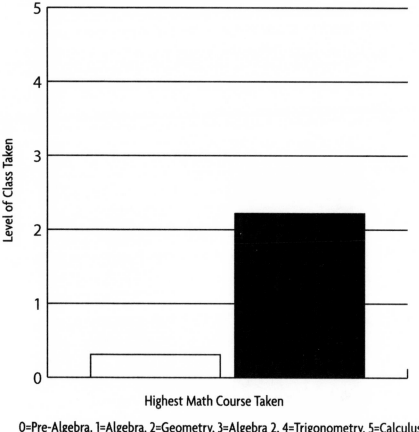

Highest Math Course Taken

0=Pre-Algebra, 1=Algebra, 2=Geometry, 3=Algebra 2, 4=Trigonometry, 5=Calculus

Figure 4.11. Highest Math Course Taken

slightly from 5th to 9th grade while those students that dropped out significantly decreased their language scores from 5th to 9th grade. See Figure 4.15.

Fifth grade total NCE vocabulary scores were significantly lower for high school dropouts (Average = 45.20) than for high school graduates (Average = 56.10). Interestingly, both graduates' and dropouts' vocabulary scores slightly decreased from 5th grade to 9th grade, and the gap between vocabulary scores remained relatively the same between dropouts and graduates. See Figure 4.16.

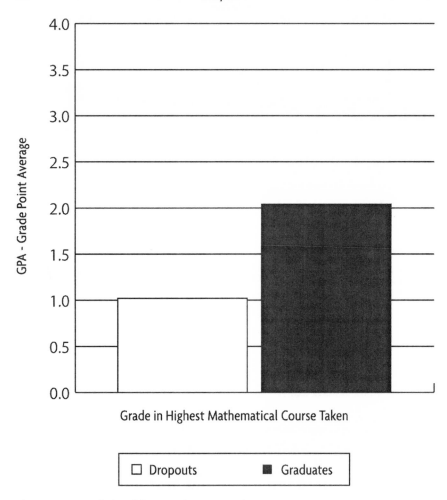

Figure 4.12. Grade in Highest Math Course Taken

Fifth grade total NCE comprehension and critical analysis scores were significantly lower for high school dropouts (Average = 44.94) than for high school graduates (Average = 51.91). Not only did differences exist in 5th grade between high school graduates and dropouts, but the gap also widened as students progressed from 5th grade to 9th grade. Moreover, those students that graduated slightly increased their comprehension and critical analysis scores from 5th to 9th grade while those students that dropped out significantly decreased their comprehension and critical analysis scores from 5th to 9th grade. See Figure 4.17.

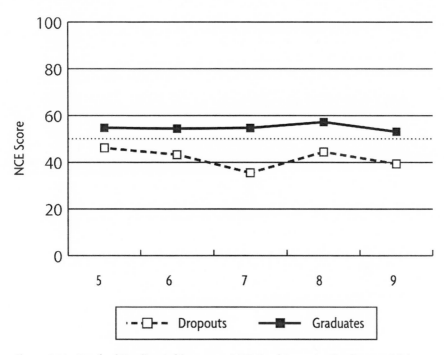

Figure 4.13. Stanford Reading Achievement (NCE Total Scores)—Grades 5–9 (Hickman et al. [2008]. © Taylor & Francis Ltd, reprinted by permission of publisher)

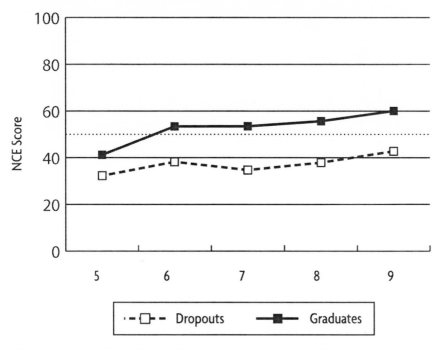

Figure 4.14. Stanford Mathematical Achievement (NCE Total Math Scores)—Grades 5–9 (Hickman et al. [2008]. © Taylor & Francis Ltd, reprinted by permission of publisher)

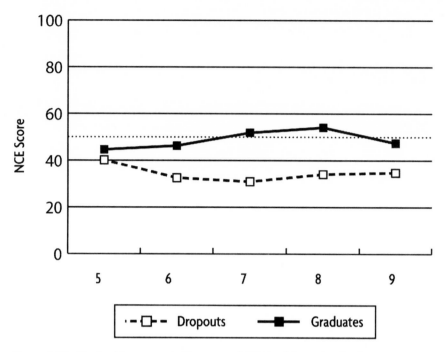

Figure 4.15. Stanford Language Achievement (NCE Total Scores)—Grades 5–9

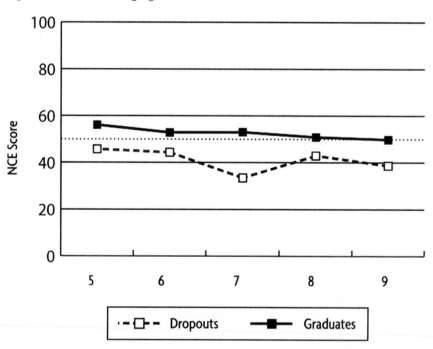

Figure 4.16. Stanford Comprehensive and Critical Analysis (NCE Total Scores)—Grades 5–9

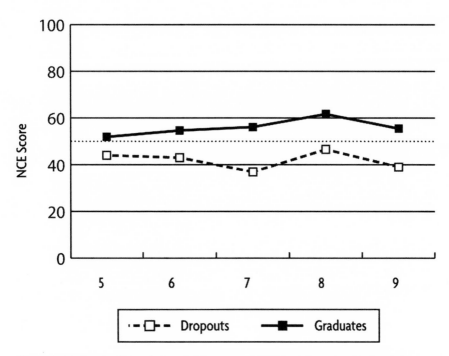

Figure 4.17. Stanford Vocabulary Achievement (NCE Total Scores)—Grades 5–9

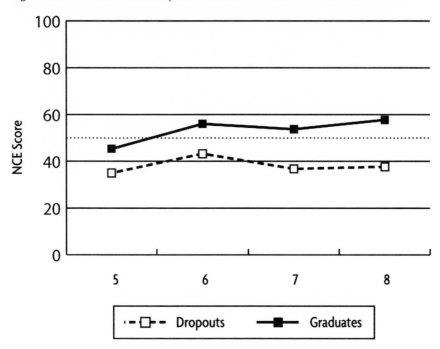

Figure 4.18. Stanford Problem-Solving Strategies Achievement (NCE Total Scores)—Grades 5–9

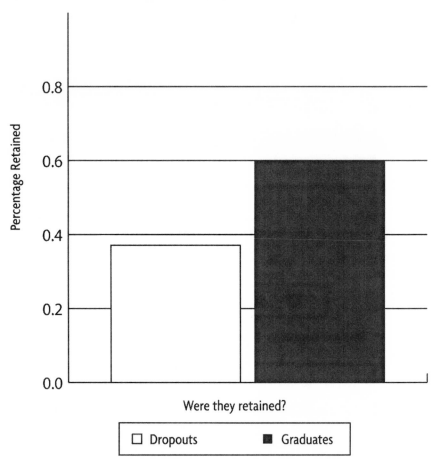

Figure 4.19. Grade Retention—Grades K–8

Fifth grade total NCE problem-solving scores were significantly lower for high school dropouts (Average = 35.00) than for high school graduates (Average = 45.34). Not only did differences exist in 5th grade between high school graduates and dropouts, but the gap also widened as students progressed from 5th grade to 8th grade. Moreover, those students that graduated increased their problem-solving scores slightly from 5th to 8th grade while those students that dropped out significantly decreased their problem-solving scores from 5th to 8th grade. No records of total NCE problem-solving scores were obtained in 9th grade. See Figure 4.18.

Grade Retention. To explore grade retention, we examined student records to see if students passed each specific grade and were moved forward to the next grade. If the students passed and were moved forward, we coded them as Yes = 1; if students did not pass a specific grade and were not moved forward, we coded them as No = 0. Our study found significant differences in grade retention between high school dropouts and graduates. More specifically, high school dropouts were significantly more likely to have been retained (38% were retained) compared to high school graduates (6% were retained). See Figure 4.19. With a value of 1 being retained you can see almost all dropouts (Average = .94) were retained at least once.

John Locke is famous for his notion that children are born *tabula rasa*, or with a blank slate. That is, children can be molded to achieve a variety of developmental outcomes. However, this study clearly suggests that children are not *tabula rasa* when they arrive in kindergarten. Furthermore, it appears that students do not deviate from the developmental pathway set forth from kindergarten. As students' developmental progression unfolds, not only do they continue down the pathway they established early on, but they also become more entrenched in their current developmental progression, regardless of the pathway. Consequently, children's academic developmental pathways tend to continue and end as started in kindergarten. Perhaps such findings lend credibility to Sigmund Freud's notion that the first five years of life comprise a critical period for child development from which all further development ensues.

Chapter 5

Absenteeism

As can be seen in Chapter 4, those students who will eventually drop out of high school come to kindergarten very differently across our study's indicators than those students who will eventually graduate from high school. In others words, as early as kindergarten children who will eventually drop out of high school are behind across academic, personal, and family factors compared to those children who will eventually graduate high school.

Such findings raise many questions. Are these observed issues a result of genetics, learning issues, family factors, demographic and/or socioeconomic factors, personal factors, poor student-teacher interactions, the school system, curricula, and/or other factors? Or are they a combination thereof? Regardless of the answer, parents, educational, political, community, and business leaders, as well as the general public, may be left wondering how or why success or failure in kindergarten sets in motion a similar developmental pathway. Why do those developmental pathways of success or failure stay the same throughout a child's schooling? Again, keep in mind that the statistical analyses presented in text, tables, and figures in this chapter are based on the 119 students (60 graduates and 59 dropouts) of our sample.

WHAT WE FOUND

When searching for answers as to why children drop out of high school, perhaps absenteeism should be discussed as a critical predictor. Absenteeism seems to be a relevant and underlying factor in related dropout research.

The findings of this study support what is already known about absenteeism. Furthermore, our research supports what is known about how

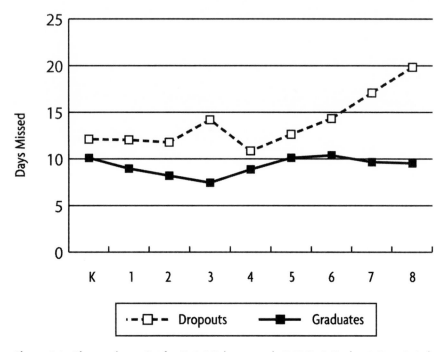

Figure 5.1. Absenteeism—Grades K–8 (Hickman et al. [2008]. © Taylor & Francis Ltd, reprinted by permission of publisher)

absenteeism affects academic success. As can be seen in Figure 5.1, as early as kindergarten, differences existed between graduates and dropouts; namely, dropouts missed more school than graduates, although not significantly until 1st grade. From 1st grade the differences between dropouts' and graduates' absenteeism remained statistically significant through 8th grade.

This pattern not only held true over time, but the gap regarding absenteeism between dropouts and graduates increased over time. Dropouts were absent approximately 20% more days in kindergarten than graduates. By the time students were in 8th grade, dropouts were absent approximately 108% more days than graduates. Interestingly, the developmental pathway of absenteeism for graduates did not vary much from kindergarten through 8th grade; graduates continued to miss approximately 9–10 days a year compared to dropouts who missed almost 20 days per year by the time they reached 8th grade. Indeed, the largest statistical difference between graduates and dropouts in this study was 8th grade absenteeism.

Perhaps even more startling is that dropouts missed approximately 124 days of school between kindergarten and 8th grade. On the surface, this finding may not appear to be such a large figure, given nine years of

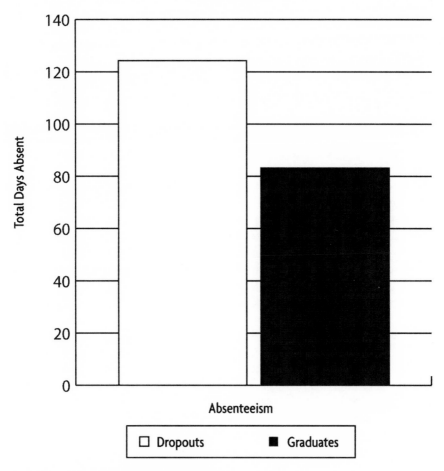

Figure 5.2. Total Days Absent—Grades K–8

schooling. However, since a typical school year consists of about 180 days, dropouts are missing just short of one academic school year in seat time and instructional guidance during their first nine years of school. Indeed, not one student in this study who missed the average absenteeism mark of dropouts at any given grade level graduated from high school. In other words, once on the path of dropping out, children stayed on that path of dropping out because they seemingly could not manage to overcome the gaps of instruction that are part of missing almost a full year of school. See Figure 5.2.

Although this research is useful for understanding the statistical relationship between absenteeism and dropping out of high school, there are more reasons linking absenteeism and dropping out of high school. For example, according to the National Dropout Prevention Center, children and families who experience absenteeism usually categorically fall into one or more of the following:

1. *Problems at school and/or at home.* These children are described as children who have disengaged from others in families and/or schools. Such children tend to experience heightened family conflict and/or have been home schooled in efforts to disengage from local school systems.
2. *Intermittent multi-dimensional disengagement.* These are children and families described as encountering temporary periods of poverty, homelessness, troubled family relationships, and/or health problems.
3. *Continuous multi-dimensional disengagement.* Such children and families are described as having enduring, long-lasting negative life events. These problems occur across settings, repeatedly, and over a lifetime.

Interestingly, most of these circumstances surrounding absenteeism tend to be found in circumstances outside of the control of schools; yet school administrators and staff members seek to increase student attendance with mixed results. Charlotte Danielson's research-based best school practices addresses attendance problems by suggesting that rigid attendance and tardy policies are punitive and do not usually result in student success. Rather, when these policies focus on optimizing attendance and learning, and are adaptive to circumstance combined with student input, there are increased opportunities for student success. From a systems perspective, shifting from one-size-fits-all "accountability" approaches to engaging related student factors promotes clearer understanding—and improved student and parent engagement.

Recent research by the National Center for Children in Poverty explored why children in high poverty areas tend to be chronically absent. The Center's findings suggest that school staff members fail to: (a) communicate the importance of attendance to parents in their home language and in culturally appropriate ways; (b) reach out to families when children miss extended periods; (c) engage parents in their children's education; and (d) offer high-quality, engaging, and safe educational experiences for children.

Other findings suggest that children who are chronically absent tend to live in families that move often, lack resources to clothe, feed, and provide educational tools for their children, and have a history of negative experiences with educational systems. Finally, research finds that children who experience chronic absenteeism encounter communities with inadequate educational resources such as preschool and daycare, lack informal and formal social supports from a variety of community agencies, and experience communities associated with high levels of violence and social disorganization.

Final Thoughts on Absenteeism

As can be seen, there is an abundance of research addressing school absenteeism. The statistical findings from our study on absenteeism are helpful for understanding the developmental pathway of children who exhibit "dropout" behaviors. Such research should help educators and other interested parties to hearken back in time at earlier grade levels, look at trends, and examine the variation in attendance. As seen in Figure 5.2, graduates vary little from year to year in their levels of absenteeism. Such an approach enables educators and other interested parties to have knowledge of and make predictions based on past and current data. Statistical findings presented in this book should help educators and other interested parties to identify children who are missing school at a rate similar to those children who dropped out of school. By identifying these children, educators and others can begin to explore the background and circumstance of the chronically absent child and consider intervention options. Understanding some of the additional research can help educators and others to understand the *system* children encounter, which is ultimately negatively affecting their educational development.

High school dropouts have insights that can contribute to our understanding. Every year the authors of this book gather together high school dropouts from around the state of Arizona to conduct the Arizona High School Town Hall. We ask these adolescents to provide the reasoning behind why they dropped out of high school. Common answers include pregnancy, suspensions, expulsions, incarceration, migrant families, and working to support families. But what is most the common issue? Absenteeism. Further, such factors are not always directly linked to educational systems.

Although many adolescents return to school despite these and other barriers, when these students do return to school, they find themselves academically behind their peers as a result of missing educational guidance and instruction. As a result of their educational gaps, these students begin to disengage even further from school as they realize they are simply too far behind to catch up to their peers. As you will read in Chapter 8, school staff members usually attempt to correct such students' academic gaps by enrolling and re-enrolling them in difficult core courses for remediation. Ultimately, the excessive absenteeism that played a significant role in producing their academic gaps drives a wedge between the students and the school. The result is that these students drop out of high school.

Chapter 6

Middle School

When we first began the process of this study, we heard, "I can't tell you exactly what age they [dropouts and graduates] will begin to look different, but I can tell you that the gap between the two [dropouts and graduates] will be most pronounced during junior high or middle school." This is right.

WHAT WE FOUND

In Chapter 3 we show that children who will eventually drop out of high school look different in all areas as early as kindergarten when compared to children who will eventually graduate from high school. In Chapter 4, our research clearly illustrates the early struggles children who eventually dropped out of school encountered in the education system. Also, the dropout path became more pronounced as children progressed from the early elementary years to the junior high or middle school years. This gap between dropouts and graduates became so significantly different that we had to alter our statistical analysis in this study. We mentioned that we compared average values between graduates and dropouts for each subject/course at each grade level from kindergarten through 12th grade or at the point of dropping out. The statistical procedure for comparing averages of two groups, like graduates and dropouts, is t-tests. In short, t-tests are used when comparing similar groups. The thought behind this approach is that differences between groups are thought to be the outcome (subject/course grade) instead of differences within the groups. However, by the time future dropouts and graduates reached middle school, they no longer resembled one another. In a statistical sense, by middle school dropouts were already dropping out—they may have been in school physically, but they were not in school academically.

A closer look at the figures presented in Chapter 4 shows that the biggest differences between dropouts and graduates in this study can be seen in 8th grade course performance, across the board, and absenteeism. While this could lead some to say, "OK, then, if 8th grade is when the biggest gap between dropouts and graduates occurs, then let's focus efforts in middle school/junior high so we can get them back on the path." The problem with this approach is that such cause-and-effect thinking overlooks the human ecology of current, recent, and past history. Such a thought is a common do-something fallacy. Educators and policy- and decision-makers assume that children operate or develop in an "educational vacuum"; they don't consider the students' complete academic, behavioral, family, and demographic history.

The idea of getting these students at risk for dropping out "back on track" assumes there is an available school track (usually the same track used by graduated students) by which to reach the goal or the "end of the line" called graduation. By middle school, dropouts are so entrenched in their developmental path it has become too late for educators and other stakeholders to lock in on a linear or singular approach of getting those children "back on track." In other words, at this stage in school development, there are no "quick fixes" or "magic bullets" that can repair the child or alter the developmental track that ends with dropping out of school.

Unfortunately, many educators and stakeholders hold the belief that everyone can succeed and graduate from high school despite clear evidence that suggests differently. Let's take a closer look at this assumption of identifying children at risk for dropping out of high school and getting them "back on track." As was the procedure in the previous chapters, the statistical analyses presented in text, tables, and figures presented in this chapter are based on the 119 students (60 graduates and 59 dropouts) of our sample.

Math Performance

As illustrated in Figure 6.1, 1st grade dropouts had an average math GPA of 2.67 while graduates had an average GPA of 3.49. As early as 1st grade, graduates' math performance was about 23.5% higher than that of children who eventually dropped out of school. Interestingly, both dropouts' and graduates' math performance declined during the elementary and middle school period. By 8th grade, the average math GPA for dropouts had decreased to 1.25 while graduates' average math GPA had decreased to 2.33. When compared to graduates, dropouts' average math performance had worsened by about 46.4% by 8th grade.

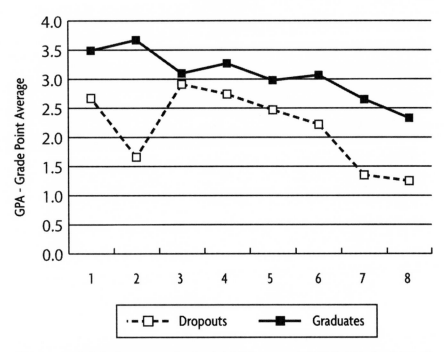

Figure 6.1. Math Performance—Grades 1–8 (Hickman et al. [2008]. © Taylor & Francis Ltd, reprinted by permission of publisher)

Reading Performance

As shown in Figure 6.2, 1st grade dropouts had an average reading GPA of 2.66 compared to an average reading GPA of 3.61 for graduates. As early as 1st grade, future graduates' reading performance was about 26.4% higher than that of children who eventually dropped out of school. As was the case in mathematical performance, both dropouts' and graduates' reading performance declined during the elementary and middle school period. By 8th grade dropouts' average reading GPA had decreased to 1.95 while graduates' average reading GPA had decreased to 2.85. When compared to future graduates' reading performance, future dropouts' average reading performance had decreased by about 31.5% by 8th grade.

English Performance

As illustrated in Figure 6.3, in 1st grade future dropouts had an average English GPA of 2.67 while future graduates had an average English GPA of 3.46. As early as 1st grade, future graduates' reading performance was about

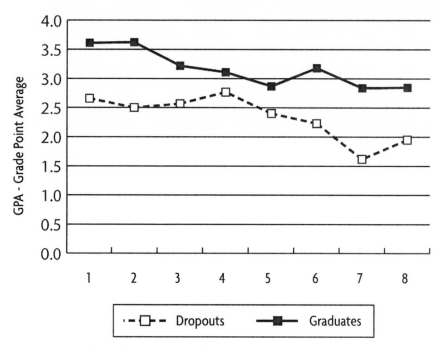

Figure 6.2. Reading Performance—Grades 1–8 (Hickman et al. [2008]. © Taylor & Francis Ltd, reprinted by permission of publisher)

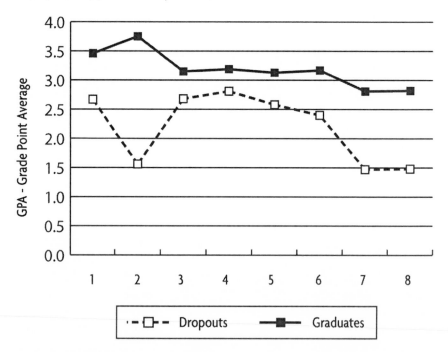

Figure 6.3. English Performance—Grades 1–8 (Hickman et al. [2008]. © Taylor & Francis Ltd, reprinted by permission of publisher)

22.9% higher than that of children who eventually dropped out of school. As was the case in math and reading performance, dropouts' and graduates' English performance declined during the elementary and middle school period. Moreover, by 8th grade future dropouts' average English GPA had decreased to 1.48 while future graduates' average English GPA had decreased to 2.82. When compared to future graduates' average English GPA, future dropouts' average English GPA had decreased by about 48.7% by 8th grade.

Social Studies Performance

As shown in Figure 6.4, in 2nd grade future dropouts had an average social studies GPA of 2.00 while future graduates had an average social studies GPA of 3.00. As early as 2nd grade, future graduates' average social studies performance was about 33.3% higher than that of children who eventually dropped out of school. As was the case in math, reading, and English performance, future dropouts' and graduates' performance in social studies declined during the elementary and middle school period. Moreover, by 8th grade future dropouts' social studies average GPA had decreased to 1.05

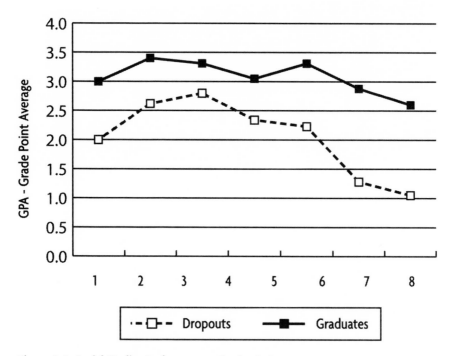

Figure 6.4. Social Studies Performance—Grades 2-8

compared to graduates' average social studies GPA, which had decreased to 2.60. When compared to future graduates' average social studies GPA, future dropouts' average social studies GPA had decreased by about 59.5% by 8th grade.

Science Performance

As illustrated in Figure 6.5, in 2nd grade future dropouts had an average science GPA of 2.50 compared to future graduates' average science GPA of 4.00. As early as 2nd grade, future graduates' average science performance was about 37.5% higher than that of children who eventually dropped out of school. As was the case with math, reading, English, and social studies performance, future dropouts' and graduates' performance in science declined during the elementary and middle school period. Moreover, by 8th grade, future dropouts' average science GPA had decreased to 1.63 compared to future graduates' average science GPA, which had decreased to 2.70. When compared to future graduates' science GPA, future dropouts' average science GPA had decreased by about 39.6% by 8th grade.

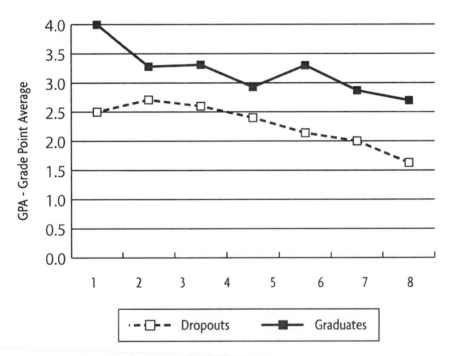

Figure 6.5. Science Performance—Grades 2–8

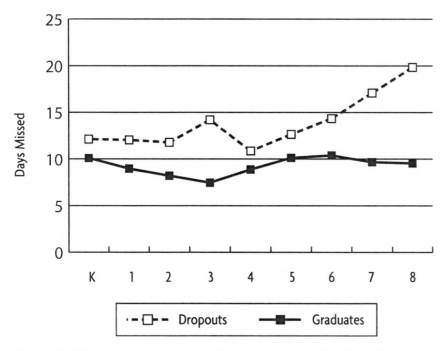

Figure 6.6. Absenteeism—Grades K–8 (Hickman et al. [2008]. © Taylor & Francis Ltd, reprinted by permission of publisher)

Absenteeism

As shown in Figure 6.6, in kindergarten future dropouts missed on average 12.13 days of school while future graduates missed on average 10.10 days. As early as kindergarten, future dropouts were missing about 16.7% more days per school year than future graduates. During the elementary and middle school period, future dropouts tended to miss more and more school, while future graduates improved their attendance slightly. By 8th grade future dropouts missed on average 19.84 days of school per year while future graduates missed on average 9.54 days of school per year. Thus, by 8th grade future dropouts were missing about 51.9% more days of school per year than future graduates. See Table 6.1 for an overview of the educational developmental progression from elementary to middle school for future dropouts and graduates.

When we examined the data shown in the figures in this chapter, we noticed that, in some instances, such as in math and English performance, future dropouts performed particularly poorly in 2nd grade while future graduates simultaneously, and significantly, increased their performance. We also noticed that future dropout and graduate performance was very similar in 3rd grade but, from 4th grade to 8th grade, the gap or deficit between future dropouts and graduates increased.

Why does this apparent trend occur? Perhaps the reasoning is connected to the grading system in 1st grade. At this point the majority of students get written performance evaluations and scoring along "Satisfactory," "Needs Improvement," and "Unsatisfactory." In 2nd grade, when all students have GPAs, the gap between math and English performance of future dropouts and graduates dramatically increases. Perhaps the shift toward grades and GPAs in the 2nd grade just makes the difficulties future dropouts experience more apparent because dropouts were already behind graduates in kindergarten and 1st grade. By 3rd grade, after a year of being on a grading scale, perhaps children became familiar with grading policies and had adapted. This may explain why those children who would eventually drop out caught up to their peers who would eventually graduate. Indeed, by 3rd grade future dropouts had narrowed the deficit in math performance from about 23.5% in 1st grade to about 6.2% by 3rd grade, and they had narrowed the English performance deficit of 22.9% in 1st grade to about 16.0% by 3rd grade. However, from 4th grade to 8th grade, the downward spiral of decreasing dropout performance became significantly worse compared to graduates during this five-year developmental period. See Table 6.1 for a summary of subject/course performance from 1st to 8th grades.

These findings suggest that future graduates and dropouts follow significant developmental trends or pathways across subjects and courses. With this information in mind, we find the notion of getting students "back on track" is not the solution to the dropout problem. Simply addressing issues of academic performance or absenteeism in the 8th grade in isolated, singular ways will not accomplish getting future dropouts "back on track" because, clearly, dropouts have never been "on track." The research findings show problems

Table 6.1. Summary of Subject/Course Performance—Grades 1–8

Subject	Dropout 1st Grade	Graduate 1st Grade	Percentage Difference	Dropout 8th Grade	Graduate 8th Grade	Percentage Difference
Math	2.67	3.49	23.50%	1.25	2.33	46.40%
Reading	2.66	3.61	26.40%	1.95	2.85	31.50%
English	2.67	3.46	22.90%	1.48	2.82	48.70%
Social Studies*	2.00	3.00	33.30%	1.05	2.60	59.50%
Science*	2.50	4.00	37.50%	1.63	2.70	39.60%
Absenteeism	12.13	10.10	16.70%	19.84	9.54	51.90%

*Denotes 2nd–8th grade comparisons

leading to dropping out started in kindergarten and lasted throughout elementary and middle school years.

Let us look at this problem of getting future dropouts "back on track" from a different angle. If we could get youth to improve attendance, would this, in turn, improve math performance in 8th grade? For the sake of argument, let's say that decreasing absenteeism improved math performance in any given grade. However, would that improve parental education? Would that decrease family barriers? Would that change or alter family structure? Would that decrease eligibility rates for free and/or reduced lunch (by increasing family income)? Would that decrease family mobility or community crime or increase community support? Would that increase involvement in extracurricular activities or reduce behavioral problems? Finally, if we improved or decreased any one of the aforementioned "usual suspects," would that get future dropouts "back on track"? The answer is no.

This pathway of dropping out of school that started in kindergarten became further entrenched in 4th–6th grades, and becomes circumstance that is beyond a linear, cause-and-effect approach to solving at the end of 8th grade. Furthermore, add in the "usual suspects" that the dropouts in this study usually encountered (such as negative life events, low family income, high family mobility, low parental education, English as a second language, high absenteeism, Title I services, FRL services, special education services, lack of participation in extracurricular activities, behavioral problems, and early identification in life as being a problem child), and you have the recipe for a child dropping out of school. This situation needs more comprehensive strategies than those involved in just getting a child "back on track."

Chapter 7

Core Courses

As we have clearly shown, the developmental pathways of graduates and dropouts are distinct and divergent. Those children who will eventually drop out of high school come to "the table" or kindergarten already behind those children who will eventually graduate. Further, future dropouts' developmental pathway gap becomes increasingly larger during middle school to the point that dropouts no longer resemble graduates.

What do we do with children, already on the pathway of dropping out of school, who have never been equal with children who are on the pathway to graduating? As you have seen, these children began at a disadvantage in kindergarten and fell even further behind their peers as they transitioned from 8th grade to high school.

First, educators have created "bridge" programs to help ease the transition from 8th to 9th grade. This effort is supposed to help adolescents prepare for the rigors of high school so they can adapt to their new school surroundings and rigorous academics. Initially, the idea of a bridge program sounds like the right thing to do. Do these programs hurt? Bridge programs are usually "one-size-fits-all," instead of being tailored for specific youth with certain types of behaviors and facing certain types of barriers. One-size-fits-all programs are designed to be similar to an inoculation. That is, everyone receives the same "Life in High School" approach or *treatment* in an effort to prevent undesirable outcomes, such as not adapting to high school. The problem with one-size-fits-all approaches such as 8th-to-9th grade bridge programs is that these appear to only benefit those children who are responsive to similar middle-of-the road schooling practices. Top-performing youth tend to adapt and succeed regardless of such programs, but those youth who struggle and perform at the bottom percent of their classes tend not to adapt or succeed regardless of *fix* or *repair* programs. For those youth who value schooling as the system is, specialized programs for succeeding in schools lack relevance. Hence, programming focused on helping students transition from 8th to 9th grade appears to waste money, time, and effort. Our study indicates graduates succeed and dropouts fail regardless of a bridge program.

Also, the idea behind 8th-to-9th grade bridge programs is that those supported youth need a gentle nudge or push in the right direction. However, as can be seen in our study, youth who are on the path of dropping out need far more than a nudge, push, or bridge to get them prepared for high school. They need much more intensive programs that are tailored specifically to their needs and circumstances. In this case, school staff members and other stakeholders need to constructively examine these at-risk youth's academic, family, and behavior histories and, where possible, expectations for increasing chances for subsequent success in school. Indeed, our study clearly demonstrates that children could benefit much more from kindergarten–to–1st grade bridge programs than waiting until the transition from 8th to 9th grade; yet even this approach's success would be doubtful because dropouts present challenging and complicated issues that tend to defy one-size-fits-all remedies. While remediation is a common school staff response (with support from a number of parents and politicians), such an approach is counterproductive for high school students who are struggling.

We make students on the dropout pathway take more and more rigorous and demanding courses. Because children in 8th grade on the path of dropping out of school are so far behind, educators and, sometimes, parents place these youth in rigorous and demanding core courses to help "remediate" them, "get them up to speed," and get them "back on track" for meeting demands of future required courses and state exit exams they need to pass to graduate from high school.

WHAT WE FOUND

The term "remediation" is used by educators who assume children are familiar with course materials but simply need to "relearn" or "practice" using the materials. In our study, those on the pathway of dropping out of school were forced to "get up to speed" as they took approximately six core courses their freshman year, compared to future graduates who took approximately four core courses their freshman year. See Figure 7.1.

It seems counterintuitive that dropouts would take more rigorous core courses than graduates their freshman year of school. One would think that, if children are in danger of dropping out of school, educators would make

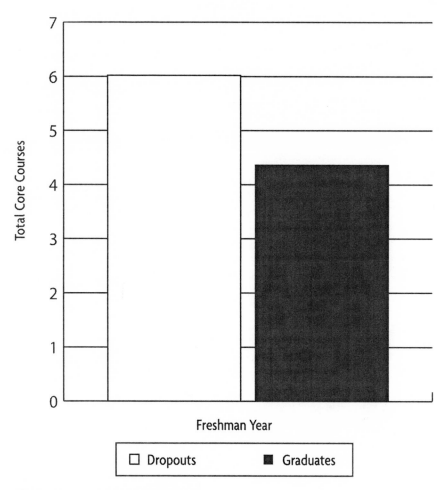

Figure 7.1. Core Courses Freshman Year

attempts to help these youth by offering classes they would like and be successful at as opposed to "throwing the book" at them, so to speak, by making them take rigorous courses to "remediate" them, "get them up to speed," or get them "back on track." What would make educators think, given historical academic and behavioral pathways of dropouts, that these children will suddenly get it together and perform acceptably? With the remediation approach in mind, many educators offer the same instruction over and over, assuming that those at risk of dropping out will eventually show some energy, not make poor choices about completing school work, and stop being lazy. Nothing about the entire academic history of those children who eventually drop out suggests that this approach would yield positive outcomes.

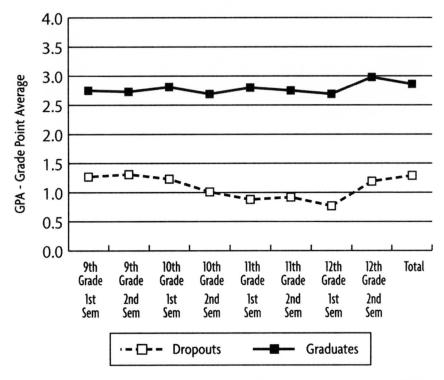

Figure 7.2. High School Academic Performance—Grades 9–12 (Hickman et al. [2008]. © Taylor & Francis Ltd, reprinted by permission of publisher)

What happens next is that those youth who are at risk of dropping out become completely disengaged from formal school learning. All educators and interested stakeholders have to do is to look at the first semester of the 9th grade year to predict academic outcomes in terms of GPA. As you can see, there is almost no variation from the 9th grade first semester forward, regardless of whether adolescents drop out or graduate. See Figure 7.2.

By high school, not only did future dropouts perform even more poorly than they had in the past, but many also began to engage in problem behaviors that introduced them to the juvenile justice system. For example, future dropouts entered the juvenile justice system at an earlier age than future graduates and were assigned to more diversion programs, put on probation, and subjected to intense probation more often than graduates. See Figure 7.3.

Educators face the problem of what to do with youth who come to 9th grade so far behind their peers that will eventually graduate. Because of No Child Left Behind and state-mandated exit exams in many states, educators are forced to get these kids "back on track." But, as you can see in our

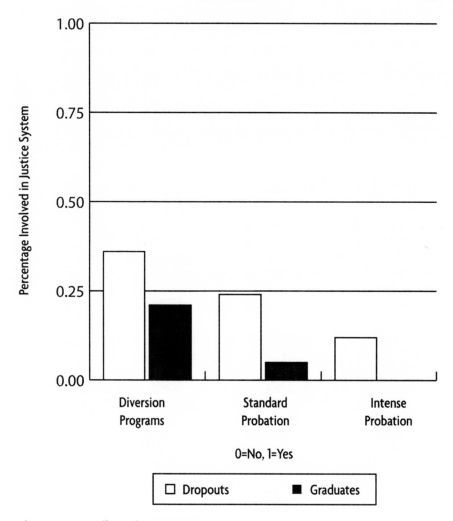

Figure 7.3. Juvenile Justice System Data

study, dropouts were never "on track." How is forcing more demanding and rigorous courses as a matter of institutional and mechanized thinking going to get such students "back on track" at this point? Ultimately, such attempts by educators, parents, and other stakeholders backfire because these children drop out, on average, in 10th grade.

If educators and other stakeholders could have taken the time to find ways to engage those students who were at risk of dropping out through personally relevant and engaging courses, perhaps those students would have found value and persevered. What makes educators and other stakeholders think that when these children start differently than graduates in kindergarten, and become further behind throughout their school career though 8th grade, that somehow these children will "turn it around," "get focused," or get "back on track" in high school? Have parents, educators, and other stakeholders not seen the "writing on the wall" and the probable outcome of dropping out of school for years?

Youth drop out of school for several reasons. First, many educators fail to recognize the academic, family, and behavioral pathways of children from the student's perspective throughout his or her time in school. Second, educators and stakeholders rely on underdeveloped programs aimed at high school-aged students to keep children from dropping out of school. Third, the literacy-only and grade retention approaches undertaken by educators, parents, and stakeholders for kindergarten and early elementary-aged students do not work past often short-term results. Fourth, educators, parents, and stakeholders taking a here-and-now approach seek to get adolescents "back on track" through remediating—offering the same instruction over and over. Fifth, educators, parents, and stakeholders assume a straight-line, cause-and-effect approach of any given mentoring or remediation program will get youth "back on track" without considering the complexities that come with a particular student's family, behavioral, and academic history. Last, those who are engaged in educating youth may not understand the human ecology of children and how multiple and influential systems operate in starting and propelling youth down the developmental pathway toward dropping out of school.

Chapter 8

Standardized Tests vs. Classroom Performance

How many times have you heard someone say, "I don't get it—my child has so much more ability than the way he/she is performing in class"? How many teachers have told parents during parent-teacher conferences that their children are not performing up to their abilities in the classroom?

Would you be surprised at this point in the book that dropouts do not perform up to their abilities? Would you be surprised that graduates do perform up to their abilities? Although the answer to both questions is usually yes, there is an interesting finding that deserves further exploration in order to learn more about dropouts.

First, we need to discuss what is meant by standardized tests and classroom performance. Standardized tests, such as the Stanford Achievement Tests used in this study, are developed by using a great number of different types of students across the United States to help understand what should be expected as normal performance in a variety of school subjects. One way to see how this looks is to use the bell curve distribution of student scores. For example, people's average intellectual quotient (IQ) is 100, with most people scoring a little higher or lower in a range—we use a standard deviation of 15 to capture this—so average IQ scores for about 68% of the population fall between 85 and 115. About 27% of people have poor or strong IQ scores (70–85 or 115–130, respectively). For most of the remaining population (about 4%), we see IQ scores that are either extremely low (55–70) or extremely high (130–145). See Figure 8.1.

In the case of Stanford Achievement Tests, children scoring above 50 are above the national average. Children scoring above 90 are scoring in the top percentage in the country compared to their peers taking the same test on the same subject.

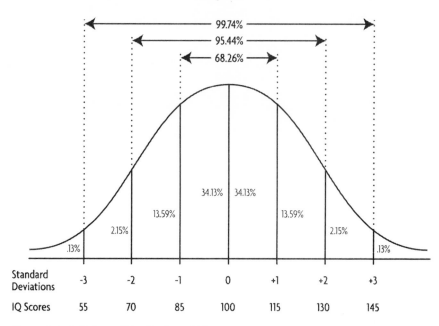

Figure 8.1. Bell Curve Distribution of IQ

Knowing student grades by courses and subjects can be helpful for comparing student, teacher, and school performance. Such comparisons are helpful for understanding overall and specific performance by student, course, subject, teacher, and grade level across similar groups. Hence, a child earning an A in 5th grade mathematics may not translate to scoring at or above national averages on 5th grade mathematical standardized tests. Why? The small numbers of students we find in classrooms will usually result in broader scoring than what we would find in standardized achievement scores. We end up with confusing measures for comparisons.

Given the apples-to-oranges comparisons between national averages and individual/small group performance scores, how can we tell if a child is performing better on standardized tests or in the classroom? How can we make sense of these two scores together? Can we get apples-to-apples comparisons? We were able to make this apples-to-apples comparison. While explaining how we derived these comparisons is beyond the scope of this book, we were able to use a statistical method to determine Z scores and, thus, compare student course grades and standardized test scores in meaningful ways.

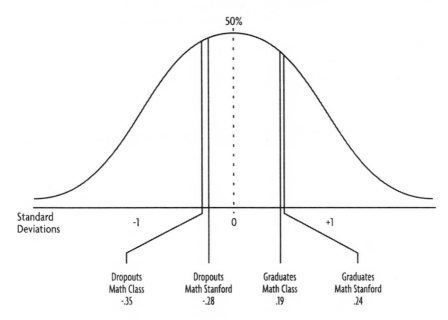

Figure 8.2. 5th Grade Standardized Values of SAT vs. Classroom Performance

WHAT WE FOUND

In our study we found that in 5th grade, future dropouts obtained a standardized score of −.28 on the mathematical component of the Stanford Achievement Test whereas future graduates obtained a .19 standardized score on the same component of the test. However, in actual classroom mathematical performance, dropouts obtained a standardized value of −.35 while graduates obtained a .24. See Figure 8.2.

By 8th grade, dropouts obtained a standardized score of −.57 on the mathematical component of the Stanford Achievement tests, whereas graduates obtained a .30 on the same test. However, in their actual classroom mathematical performance, dropouts obtained a standardized value of −.73 while graduates obtained a .29. See Figure 8.3.

Translation: Dropouts performed slightly lower in the classroom compared to their standardized testing ability in 5th grade math, while graduates performed slightly higher in the classroom compared to their standardized testing ability. Over time, graduates continued to achieve at the same levels on standardized tests and course grades, while dropouts achieved significantly less in the classroom compared to their standardized test scores. Not only did dropouts decrease in their classroom and standardized test score performances over time, but the gap between their standardized test scores or

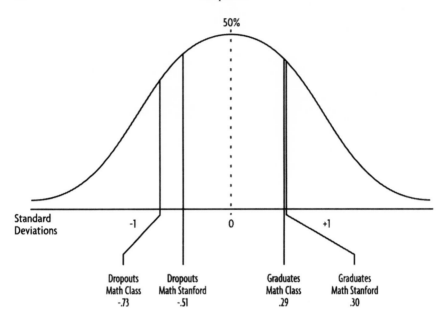

50%

Standard
Deviations   -1   0   +1

Dropouts   Dropouts   Graduates   Graduates
Math Class   Math Stanford   Math Class   Math Stanford
-.73   -.51   .29   .30

Figure 8.3. 8th Grade Standardized Values of SAT vs. Classroom Performance

ability and their classroom grades or performance also indicated that dropouts *increasingly underperformed in classrooms.*

The question is, why? Why do dropouts continue to perform more poorly in the classroom setting compared to their abilities? Or, said differently, why do dropouts fail to perform in the classroom setting when they have more ability than their course performance would indicate? This is important because the answer to the question of "Can they perform" is "Yes," but the answer to the question of "Do or will they perform" is "No." Dropouts have the ability to achieve, but they are failing to tap into their abilities to perform in school.

Perhaps this issue comes partly from the schooling process. Most teachers make assumptions about students at the beginning of the school year. Such educators and other stakeholders are quick to label youth as "bad apples," "slow learners," "problem children," and the like. Most teachers, parents, and other stakeholders value tests to measure student ability, and such results are often used for confirming "usual suspects" and targeting remedial efforts within existing instructional efforts. Classroom activities tend to be centered more on teacher notions of what works and less on the students', peers', and other concerned stakeholders' collaborative notions of what works. Standardized tests are often used by educators and others as benchmarks for indicating overall and sub-portion success and finger-pointing, not as clinical tools to help revise and individualize instruction. These and other approaches are centered on the logic and rationale of existing schooling systems and often separated from the complexities that arrive with each student's personal academic, family, and behavioral history or human ecology. What is the bottom line? *The fact that dropouts perform better on standardized tests than what their classroom performance would predict should alert educators and other stakeholders that poor classroom performance is deeply rooted in the student's human ecology, to include how educators work with these youth.*

Chapter 9

Are Educational Pathways Set in Stone from Kindergarten?

Our research clearly shows that dropouts appear to have different capabilities compared to graduates as early as kindergarten. Having academic gaps from the beginning of school, being retained, and missing a lot of school at different grade levels all contribute toward dropout pathways that look very different from graduate pathways. Further, the developmental pathway gap between graduates and dropouts becomes more pronounced as students mature from early childhood to adolescence.

The results of this study are disturbing. We saw that the developmental pathways children started on in kindergarten become deterministic. In other words, once children started on a developmental pathway of dropping out or graduating in kindergarten, the outcome became inevitable. This made us wonder, were there any children in kindergarten who were on the pathway of dropping out who were resilient or who "beat the odds" and actually graduated high school? Hence, we examined students on the developmental pathway of dropping out at in kindergarten at all points along their developmental progression in an effort to see if any children on the pathway of dropping out of school actually graduated high school. What factors or buffers did these students have and/or what experiences in their lives altered their developmental pathway and prevented them from dropping out of high school?

WHAT WE FOUND

Regretfully, only two of sixty children in our study who started out on the developmental pathway as dropouts in kindergarten got "back on track" or jumped track to the developmental pathway of graduates. We determined

67

such outcomes by examining dropout-specific values for each variable of this study across all grade levels to the average values of each variable across all grade levels of graduates. In other words, did dropouts ever resemble the average graduate? If so, what variable(s) and at what age(s) did this occur?

Sad to report that only two of those children on the pathway of dropping out who were retained or held back in kindergarten and 1st grade eventually got "back on track" and graduated high school. There was no other point in time or any variable that allowed dropouts to get "back on track" and resemble graduates in this study. Further, of the 20 children held back a grade in this study, only two graduated high school. One child was held back in kindergarten and the other child was held back in 1st grade. Not one child held back in any grade higher than 1st grade graduated high school. Given the small numbers of dropouts and graduates in this study, caution should be exercised in presuming that only holding children back in kindergarten and 1st grade is helpful. Two other children who were held back during elementary school years dropped out, matching research suggesting about half of those students who are retained a grade level eventually drop out of school. In our study, two of twenty, or 10%, of those retained in a grade managed to graduate—daunting odds.

The problem may be that parents, educators, and other decision-makers believe retaking coursework benefit those students by helping them to catch up with peers. What is missing in this problem is how youth who are held back begin to view their school potential. Children and adolescents, like the rest of us, find worth and standing by comparisons with others. Research suggests children and adolescents who believe they are "stupid" and not able to learn or read or do math may, in turn, not be able to do these things. Ask just about anyone who was held back a grade level in school how he or she felt about school, and we hear about related difficulties. Educators, parents, and decision-makers may inadvertently complicate this issue.

One-size-fits-all approaches do not target problem areas that may continue to get in the way of student success. Taking 1st grade or 7th grade or freshman English over again, with no changes to the instructional content, suggests that schools have offered all that students need to be successful, if those children and adolescents would just opt in. Perhaps this school-centered, middle-of-the-road way of thinking works for most children, but, as readily shown in our findings, this notion is not true for our students on the dropout pathway. The mechanized, efficient, reach-the-masses approach to instruction may not be helpful for the learner who struggles in school. School staff, parent, and decision-maker notions of student laziness and poor choices miss the point—blaming students for what a non-supportive school system may do is simply not productive.

Should children be held back to "catch up"? This approach doesn't seem to work most of the time. What should we do with children who are not prepared to succeed at the next level? Perhaps we need to start thinking less about levels of instruction that are constrained by specific sets of information and more about what we can do to help those students whose performance lies outside of the masses in ways that support rigor, relatedness, and individualized success. In Chapter 10, we turn toward how educators, parents, and decision-makers can craft such approaches.

Chapter 10

Understanding Human Ecology

A Systems Approach for Understanding Why Children Drop Out of School

This study has clearly shown that children continue down the developmental pathway they started in kindergarten. Rarely do they get "back on track" regardless of different attempts by educators and others. Why? Educators, parents, and other community leaders continue to largely focus efforts at the high school level of education rather than center their efforts at the elementary level where children's problems emerge and become persistent. Educators, parents, and community leaders do not account for the fact that children do not develop in an educational vacuum. Educators and others continue to overlook the layered, overlapping effects of "usual suspects." Despite this oversight of ignoring the "usual suspects," research clearly shows that it is the custom, rather than the exception, for dropouts to experience multiple "usual suspects" in their lives. In other words, educators and other interested parties continue to tackle the issue of children dropping out of school in a straight line, cause-and-effect fashion as opposed to taking a comprehensive, systems approach to understanding. There is no simple approach, or "magic bullet," that prevents youth from dropping out of school. Rather, educators, parents, and community leaders need to begin considering the human ecology of the various systems operating daily in the lives of each child. Only then can we begin to understand how to create solutions for dropout prevention.

UNDERSTANDING THE HUMAN ECOLOGY

The ecological theory of child development, offered by Urie Bronfenbrenner, examines the youth surrounded or embedded in multiple layers or systems, which eventually mold and shape the developing youngster. The immediate

71

system outside the developing child is the microsystem. Such singular systems include immediate or nuclear family, community or neighborhood, church, peers, and school, all of which affect child development. The child's experiences in these microsystems operate on the developing child, and create direct experiences and behaviors that the child takes to other microsystems. Thus, how children develop at home directly affects how they develop and perform at school. What the child does in his or her school microsystem directly affects the child's home microsystem. The child's neighborhood microsystem directly affects the child's school, home, and peer microsystems. These links between microsystems eventually create a larger system called the mesosystem, which directly affects child development. From a systems perspective, school is no more important for child development and educational outcomes than the home, neighborhood, church, and peers. Yet educators, parents, and community leaders usually continue to focus efforts on the child's educational microsystem when trying to understand high school dropouts.

Children also indirectly experience various systems at work called exosystems. For example, children directly experience their school or classroom microsystem. However, they do not directly experience the school or governing boards of their school. The rules, laws, and customs established for children and others at their school microsystem, which affect their development, come from a system they do not directly encounter. Another example would be the employer of the child's parents. Children do not directly experience their parents' work duties, conditions, or supervisors. However, they indirectly experience such systems as how the parents' microsystem of work affects their mood when they come home to their children. When parents are having bad days at work, they often come home and interact directly with their children in a negative manner because they are still upset from the day's events at the microsystem called their job. Finally, children are affected by the macrosystem or larger system of their country leaders, norms, customs, and rules and regulations. Many of these cultural norms become values, which the citizens adopt as their own. Such values and norms filter into the home, school, peer, and neighborhood microsystems and the media exosystem. Finally, the chronosystem is a system of time where changes occur in a child's life. For example, children witness the birth of siblings, the start of school, the onset of puberty, and so forth. All of these characteristics and more interact with the previously mentioned systems to create systematic development. See Figure 10.1.

Now, let us apply the system of human ecology to dropouts. How can educators and other interested parties solve the problem of dropouts by simply focusing on raising grades, creating bridge programs, developing before- and after-school programs, having volunteer mentors for kids, or any other

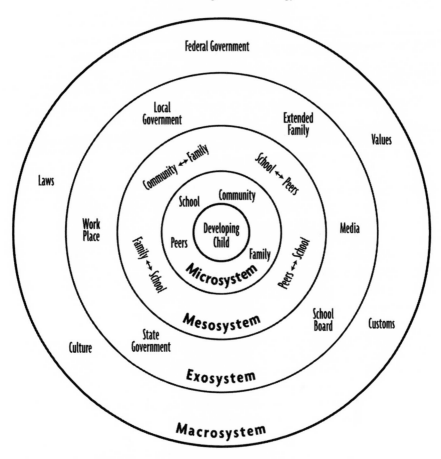

Figure 10.1. Human Ecology Model of Child Development

educational-related program at the school microsystem? What about the No Child Left Behind Act, which operates at the macrosystem? What about the media at the exosystem, which drives many of our cultural norms? What about the employers of children? What about family income and work conditions? This and a host of other issues all affect child development. Neighborhoods affect development. Peers affect development. Where schools are located in neighborhoods affect development. Teacher attitudes affect development. Parent interactions with school staff affect development. Quality of parent education affects development. The list appears endless—the systems approach suggests there is much to any given system, much more so than straight-line, cause-and-effect thinking may indicate.

How does focusing solely on education-related variables affect or change the "system" that is operating on the developing child? Raising grades or taking more core classes is the least of the child's issues at hand for those on the developmental pathway of dropping out of school. How does creating mentoring programs, after-school programs, or any other education-related attempt to work with at-risk kids alter or fix the system at large? Does it change the media? Does it change the school board rules and laws? Does it change the No Child Left Behind Act? Does it change parents' work conditions and income? Does it change the neighborhood? Does it change which kids dropouts hang out with? Does it change family-related variables such as parenting styles, discipline strategies, and family structure and mobility? As any assertive 4-year-old would say, "no." Simply focusing on education-related variables cannot change the individual's pathway of dropping out because children do not develop in an educational vacuum. By focusing on education variables alone, educators and interested parties have no chance of altering or changing the system that is creating and maintaining problems for those children on the developmental pathway of dropping out of school.

Systems Thinking

So how do we apply the systems way of thinking to understanding and working with children on the developmental pathway of dropping out of school? When considering W. Edwards Deming's total quality management (TQM) approach, we realize that human activity typically does not follow along cause-and-effect chains of events. Rather, human beings operate in complex settings with contending perspectives about how and why we do what we do. Systems thinking is about trying to understand the here-and-now *and* the future, what is occurring near us based on what is occurring elsewhere, and what we can do to improve circumstance. Systems thinking is about seeing the tree, the stand of trees, and the forest together. This type of thinking demands much deeper reflection than simply believing humans behave in straightforward, "rational" ways.

Deming's comprehensive TQM approach is useful for engaging in change strategies even in circumstances as complex as dropping out of school. The idea of this approach is to challenge existing norms and assumptions in a manner that creates information, insights, and capacities by which a system can evolve to heightened levels of development. We shall explore these three issues in turn: looking beyond symptoms, using constructive frameworks, and creating change.

Looking beyond Symptoms

What causes youth to quit school? Patterns of failure? Inability or lack of motivation to perform? Poverty? Home life? Parenting? We sense this list captures some of the sentiments of professionals and others concerned with the dropout problem. Simply reducing the dropout problem to a short list of attributes that indicates there is no need to take further action or that suggests we are not responsible for what a child chooses to do has not produced desirable change. How much of the problem lies in how we *see the problem*?

Systems thinking indicates problems are deeply ingrained in and across circumstances. To assume we can capture a problem by merely noting immediate circumstance is short-changing the fix because we tend to move from problems to fixes very quickly. Effective problem building becomes important if we hope to get the problem right, so that we can get the solution right. Perhaps an example would be helpful.

If we are working with a youth whose behavior challenges school staff, and we believe the problem is that the child is simply defiant and stubborn, what can we do? Punishment? Lecturing? Time-out? Time home (or on the streets)? If a child is naturally difficult, do we really have the means to produce a fix? Could our problem be how we are framing the problem? Does professional staff tend to isolate and locate problems as being only within the child and not caused or affected by schooling and personal practice—do we tend to blame the child instead of looking at how different systems factors may contribute to the problem? The "serenity prayer" and Julian Rotter's "locus of control" should advise us of the nearsightedness of such thinking.

> God grant me the serenity to accept the things I cannot change, the courage to change the things I can, and the wisdom to know the difference.

As we consider where we locate issues, we should be wary of attributing reasons for why youth misbehave or underperform to what is external to our control, as this leads to blame and personal angst (e.g., our wayward youth is defiant—a disposition that defies simple intervention, and rationalizes behavior and attitude over which concerned adults have no control and limited influence). If we shift across Rotter's "locus of control" to internal reasons as problems, we may be able to create or adapt approaches that are more constructive (e.g., our adventuresome youth is bored in class—can we work toward finding ways to help the student relate to the instruction by finding relevance?). Effectively framing the problem is critical for getting the problem and eventual solutions right.

Figure 10.2. Action Research Process

Action research is a systems-based approach for helping educators and other interested parties with getting the problem right, or problem building. In short, we should consider our undesirable circumstance and construct-related problems that are under educator, parent, and community control or influence. How can we do this with action research?

Action research is a process that helps practitioners dig and get the problem properly framed. In short, action research relies on different sources and research methods to understand and resolve problems through evaluation, intervention, reevaluation, and intervention, until the desired results are achieved. See Figure 10.2.

Before coming to closure about our challenging youth who frustrates school staff and others, let us do some problem building. Could the child come from a place where trust emerges very differently than it does in the mainstream school culture? How do school staff members relate to this child? Could life events at home be overpowering? What is this child's sugar intake? Is the curriculum and instruction stale, engaging few learning modes in irrelevant ways? This list could be never-ending. While solving all the maladies of the

Table 10.1 Examples of Core Problems (from Charlotte Danielson, *Enhancing Student Achievement: A Framework for School Improvement* [Alexandria, VA: ASCD], p. 59. © 2002 by ASCD. Reprinted with permission. Learn more about ASCD at www.ascd.org.)

	School Culture	Policies and Practices	Community
Wayward youth	Are students assigned to single teachers in elementary schools, single classes in high school?	Are students satisfied with just getting by?	Does school staff stipulate practices to parents and community leaders?
	Are students grouped by abilities?	Are homework policies rigid?	Does school staff or community membership avoid certain parents?
		Is there staff favoritism?	

human condition is beyond the scope of this book, what are some processes we can use to help more youth to engage in school? Considering a series of "why" questions with a focus on what we can control or influence can help identify core problems. See Table 10.1.

Table 10.1 suggests how school staff and other interested parties can do a poor job of influencing and controlling aspects of our youth's school experience. If you cannot see the connection between the challenging student and this brief list of elements of culture, policy and practice, and community, consider the following:

Single teachers and classes—Could our youth be practicing deviance partly because of power struggles or personality conflicts?

Ability grouping—Could our student feel demeaned by being with "stupid" peers?

Getting by—Could our youth be seeking a minimum level of performance?

Homework—If our student could not do the work in school, could it be done at home?

Favoritism—Does our wayward youth find others favored for positive attention?

School or community-centered policy—Does the "consequence" for a behavior make sense to our wayward youth? Do school staffs and others focus on *punishing* difficult behavior instead of teaching new behavior?

Avoidant staff or community members—Can our student detect frustration between staff, community members, and parents?

Creating effective problems in a way that offers opportunities for change is foundational to action research. To help make action research manageable, educators, parents, and community leaders would find value in relying on effective frameworks.

Using Constructive Frameworks

Charlotte Danielson's book, *Student Achievement Framework for School Improvement*, offers users an exemplary model for contrasting present and preferred practices. For example, Danielson offers her readers a rubric for contrasting policies and practices for discipline affecting students. See Table 10.2.

How do schools rate? How can educator, parent, and community leader come to know? While we will rely on Danielson's research-based approach throughout this chapter, the reader may opt for other comprehensive, research-based frameworks receiving broad support in promoting effective schooling practices. Regardless of the model used, action research helps us with coming to an understanding about the status of issues such as discipline policy.

Table 10.2. Discipline Policies

Poor	Basic	Exemplary
Standards of student conduct are arbitrary, and consequences for student infractions are punitive and harsh.	Standards of student conduct and the consequences for student infractions are reasonable.	Standards of student conduct are based on mutual respect, and consequences for student infractions are reasonable.
Discipline policies are not well publicized and students have had no opportunity to contribute to their development.	Discipline policies are publicly known and students have had some opportunity to contribute to their development.	Discipline policies are publicly known and students have contributed to their development.

Do we come to know why youth do as they do relying on rules of thumb we use to guide our own lives? How do we know that what we know is accurate, perhaps different from what we assume we know? Does our personal experience shape how we understand human nature? When we are thinking in *single loops* or straightforward, cause-and-effect ways, we tend to jump—often foolishly—from our notion of the problem to a solution. When we know our difficult child is merely disposed to be difficult, given our understanding of the defiance we are experiencing, we can resign ourselves to this circumstance. We can battle for control. We can try to punish this mind-set to help *correct* this youth's perspective. We can realize there is nothing we can do. This simply framed, single-loop problem is not well constructed, does not account for how *we* may be contributing to this issue, and does not lend itself to long-term remedy. *In fact, this kind of problem becomes self-fulfilling because we get the dispositions and behaviors we think we see based on how we treat those who have this "problem."* If we treat the defiant child as a deviant, we shall certainly find those problem behaviors and attitudes we "know" exist.

As promoted by Chris Argyris, systems thinking and action research integrates *double loops* (thinking about how we know what we know) using multiple sources and methods to try to reduce our own biases when building and engaging problems. Instead of relying solely on intuition, history, or any singular source of information filtered by a great number of assumptions and beliefs (many not known), action research helps the reflective educator or other interested party carefully develop useful problems. See Table 10.3 for an example of how we can become informed about a school's discipline policy.

This systems-thinking method tends to produce information that is more useful by offsetting different sources and ways of collecting information.

Table 10.3. Sample Action Research Findings

	Data Source #1 – Policy	Data Source #2 – Student Focus Group	Data Source #3 – Parent Survey
Discipline Policy	Policy is largely copied from administrative code with little adaptation	Student concerns appear to be focused on favoritism, inequities, lack of input	Findings suggest parents feel like recipients and not partners in school discipline issues, uneven awareness, unfair or favored disciplining

While a full explanation of action research is beyond the scope of this book, Richard Sagor's book, *Action Research*, may be a very helpful resource. What should be clear is that action research is a practical process that takes time and effort.

If you are seeking a how-to book that lists causes and effects for dropouts, you may be disappointed with this book. For the reflective educator, parent, and community leader who grasps the complexities of human behavior and disposition in sensitive ways, and is willing to engage in the hard work and critical thinking that comes with questioning personal assumptions and practices, this book holds great promise in helping you engage youth at risk of dropping out of school.

Creating Change

Framing problems in ways that offer opportunities for change is necessary to action research. For the reader who views circumstance as absolute and the children we are serving or other external factors as the problem, this may be difficult to understand. In addition to our first rule that effective action research problems have to be under our control or influence, we add that such problems need to be optimistic. The realists and naysayers may struggle with these rules, so perhaps some explanation is in order.

In overly simplified terms, we know that we have those among us who know truth as it is—the realists. These folk clearly see the world in single-loop, straightforward ways (assuming others see it the same way, or should see it the same way), and seek to continue tradition and customs because these are rational approaches that can be used to get everyone on board, going in the same direction, and understanding common truths. These realists often see change as threatening, efficiency as ideal, and student development and attitude as predictable. If you believe there always have been and will be dropouts, that some youth will always make good choices and others will not, and life is reducible to a few good rules of thumb, this book may defy common sense and not be helpful. Of course, we are not all realists stuck on current realities.

If you connect your relationships and different personal views to the truths you hold, are seeking accountability for what you can change, and grasp self-fulfilling prophesy as this relates to your own attitude, behavior, and what you *enact* in your youth (all double-loop thinking), this book holds strong promise for change. Given the usefulness of this approach, is there room for negativity? Does optimism become ethically necessary? How do we systemically create positive effective change?

First, educators, parents, and community leaders need to know where they stand and where they should be standing. The educator, parent, and community leader can accomplish this step with problem building. Initially, they can use multiple sources and research methods to establish a baseline assessment against some research-based framework that they hold as the desired performance or outcome. Second, they can invite stakeholders (other educators, parents, community leaders, even youth) to help with reviewing findings and developing interventions. This activity increases chances of gaining broad-based agreements, team building in and out of schools, homes, and communities, and creative approaches that may improve schooling. Third, the educator, parent, and community leader should again measure for improvements using action research methods with a preferred framework. As improvements occur and this process is repeated, different opportunities will emerge, shifting the focus and direction of interventions, and school staffs and other organizations will learn ways to reduce the dropout problem. Let us explore applied practices from a systems theory perspective across the five major findings of this study: kindergarten, absenteeism, middle school, core courses, and standardized vs. classroom performance.

KINDERGARTEN

We seek regular school attendance in hopes of promoting an educated citizenry. We screen our little ones to help sort out those who are school ready from those with social and emotional delays. We seek to know our children's needs in hopes of making necessary accommodations. But, as shown in our study, we have yet to realize full success in reaching those "at-risk" students in comprehensive ways.

So, what works in school participation and early intervention programs? We have laws that address parental neglect, health supports in schools, early reading- and behavior-based programs provided for students who struggle, open-door policies at schools to invite parent engagement, community support for parent days, and other approaches that still fall short of helping us reach those children most in need of our help.

Why don't these problems-to-solutions work? Well, simple and direct assumptions about why children struggle do not lead to straightforward interventions because the problems are not fully developed or understood. Offering an after-school reading program for children from impoverished homes without benefit of safe transportation does not work. Asking children to stay in school for more engaged activities when the time they already spend in school is miserable is not well received by the student (and, often, by their parents). A mainstream, middle-class culture could be considered hostile to those who do not share similar values, and educators and community leaders often promote those middle-class values.

Some research-based reading intervention programs are effective, but research shows that children who do not continue to receive those intervention services after the 3rd grade tend to relapse to prior poor performance and behavior, suggesting these programs should be considered as models for teaching larger numbers of students instead of early stopgaps. Could some of these early intervention behavioral and literacy programs work, in part, because of positive relationships between adult and children, highly adapted instruction that is personalized for relevance, and opportunities for student success? Do we offer all children this same instructional approach? Should we?

SCHOOL-BASED PROBLEMS AND SOLUTIONS

Many school staff members have their own notions of how young children ought to behave, and they think of themselves as the be-all, end-all knowledge holders of child development. This approach, when combined with linear, cause-and-effect thinking, could do more to perpetuate instead of remedying student problems. When children cannot read to level or act out inappropriately, do we now absorb educator energy that could be better spent on those children who follow our rules and can perform as we expect they should? Do we have an opportunity to stretch professionally and view circumstance in ways to help our struggling *and* mainstream youth? When we recognize a child as being lazy, could we be looking in a mirror and find that our own efforts at meeting the needs of that challenging child are coming up a bit short? Can children smile, laugh, and be playful even as they struggle with schoolwork? Should we deny them playground time to do schoolwork, thus proving that schoolwork is the punishment they believe it to be?

Should children who struggle with reading and behaviors get help? Absolutely. Should that help be based on institutional practices that perpetuate and rationalize schooling as *the* answer? Probably not. Research suggests the closer we can get to addressing student needs, the better chances we have of effecting positive change. This means the way educators and others interested in helping children often think about the problem could, in fact, *be* the problem. So, what are some practical and effective strategies, tactics, and, possibly most important, dispositions?

Teaching

Problems-turned-solutions are not constructive when educators perceive negative student and parent attitudes (e.g., teachers cannot fix lazy children or make irresponsible parents accountable). Successful problem building relies on optimistic, teacher-controlled variables and characteristics. Table 10.4 lists some examples of problems and solutions that may help with school kindergarten issues.

Administration

Principals and other administrators face mounting accountability measures for issues in and out of their control. Some respond by becoming insular to

Table 10.4. Teacher-Centered School Kindergarten Problems and Solutions

Problem	Solution	Remarks
Insensitive, one-size-fits-all classroom management	Revise singular approaches with flexible responses focusing on student learning more so than consequences; tailor responses to children	Discipline varies across homes; some parents will side with their children if they do not share similar beliefs about common schooling discipline; integrate parental input; reward positive behaviors; carefully consider and possibly revise any consequence intended to punish
Blame student for behaviors	Accepts responsibility for student success, clinically finds and acts on contributing factors	Tone, frustration, and anger can all be misconstrued by students as indicative of inferiority, given the powerful role teachers play in the lives of students; find ways to structure engaging learning and positive discipline approaches

comfortable processes that are rational for traditional school staff processes (and minimize vulnerabilities to outsider scrutiny). Others seek ways of making sense of circumstance by reviewing and perpetuating self-serving history (e.g., the parents did not do well in school; we should expect no more from their children). Addressing early literacy and behavioral issues call for different, more productive ways of thinking. Table 10.5 offers some provisional problems and solutions that may help with kindergarten issues from administrative standpoints.

COMMUNITY-BASED PROBLEMS AND SOLUTIONS

Schooling is a community issue, not just a school issue. Focusing on assigning responsibilities and holding various organizations accountable as means to improved performance is reactive and leads to finger-pointing—this overly simplistic, cause-and-effect viewpoint tends to be more destructive than constructive. While school staffs need to be nurturing and clinical in how they help those who struggle with literacy and pro-social behaviors, community leaders need to find ways to support and not shun those children and their

Table 10.5. Administrative-Centered Kindergarten Problems and Solutions

Problem	Solution	Remarks
Inflexible student rosters	Consider case managing students with propensities for absenteeism and behavior issues and, recognizing staff strengths, assign and reassign students accordingly	School youth may bond with different staff, or respond to a new and different approach
Multiple barriers based on lack of resources (e.g., transportation, food, clothing)	Coordinate with support agencies to offer support, possibly acting as central coordinating point of contact	Poverty framework involves transportation, meal, clothing barriers that regularly attending children seldom face
Site councils who do not engage critical subgroups of parents and community leaders	Find ways to attract and invite parent participation, especially those parents whose children struggle with regular attendance	Shared decision-making and collegiality promotes enfranchisement and open communications
Uneven resource allocation	Consider allocating resources for students in tiered responses; provide needy students with more resources	Reconsider fairness from equal distribution to proportionate needs; just as some children require more supports, so do their parents

families who struggle in schools and communities. Sponsoring non-punitive, family-centered fun reading events, education fairs that include positive discipline approaches, and coordinated school and community processes and supports for families at risk are helpful toward improving chances of increasing literacy and pro-social behaviors. Table 10.6 offers some tentative problems and solutions that may be helpful.

Youth who succeed in school believe they are capable of doing the work and getting along with others. Children who struggle with reading and writing label themselves as stupid—not productive. Children who struggle to get along with other children need supports to guide behavior, not punishment that reinforces the behavior. The community plays a large and sometimes direct role in coming to grips with these challenging issues.

Absenteeism

In an effort to reduce absenteeism and dropout rates, educational policy experts have created compulsory attendance laws based on age. The laws vary across states. Although requiring students in their teens to attend high school may be beneficial in lowering the dropout rate, this study demonstrated very clearly that differences in absenteeism existed as early as kindergarten. With dropouts missing on average 124 days in grades K–8, perhaps education policy should be focused on creating strategies or mandates for improving student attendance in elementary and middle grades as well.

Given the findings of our study, the question becomes, "What works in reducing absenteeism?" This question troubles educators and other interested parties at schools, in communities, across states, and nationally. Children who miss many days of school, regardless of the reason, are at risk for further academic and social problems in school. If educators and other interested parties peg children as being "at-risk" based on extensive absenteeism, they need to create suitable programs for intervention that wrap around student barriers. Research has clearly demonstrated that programs and interventions designed to reduce problem behaviors among "at-risk" children must include help from the school, family, and community because behaviors such as missing school are often entrenched across these "systems."

SCHOOL-BASED PROBLEMS AND SOLUTIONS

Institutionally centered consideration of attendance issues limits and stops opportunities for addressing attendance issues. Instituting clear attendance rules and policies, more broadly advertising school operating hours, mandating

Table 10.6. Community-Centered Kindergarten Problems and Solutions

Problem	Solution	Remarks
Lack of parent engagement/ leadership	Find ways (e.g., host dinners, honor parents) to target parents of children who struggle in schools to initiate/sustain collaborative and volunteering opportunities and share decision-making across agencies	Parent participation is critical for student success in school
Contending values	Find ways to capture insights from parents whose views differ from the norm; consider opportunities for improvement; engage community and business leaders for coherent approach for helping parents/employees support children in school activities	Community and business leader investment into school processes can manifest through direct and indirect support (e.g., employers allowing needy parents time to meet school transition needs for youth)
Myths and rumors	Communicate in multiple ways (sending written notes to illiterate parents about the importance of writing is counterproductive); foster community gatherings, including school, for addressing concerns	Employers and agency leaders should seek ways to help promote school activities and engage in related governance
Lack of community and business leader participation	Find ways to mentor youth who face barriers for success in school; support parents who face barriers with time and resources for helping ensure children are in school; participate in school governance	One-size-fits-all programs usually only meet the needs of a few students; committing time for needy youth yields higher returns than other resources
Schooling is an artificial process isolated from the community and other natural supports and resources	Find ways to integrate business, community, and school participation with service projects and internships that connect learning with doing	Curricular relevance and differentiation enrich learning experiences; getting parents and community leaders involved in learning processes promotes more unified, shared approach for youth benefit
Mixed signals/ supports for impoverished and disenfranchised families	Find ways to consolidate service support agencies and resources under single points of contact to help make systems rational and more economical, and invite school staff; operate from family assets perspective	Parents and families with students who struggle with attendance often have needs that can be met by different constellations of service approaches

attendance through coercive threats against parents and older students, and offering educational advertisement about the importance of attending school aimed at those who are probably least equipped to understand or lack access to the message will probably not improve attendance. School-housed activities immersed in school logic (e.g., "parent university—come learn how to read to your child") will generally draw parents predisposed to participate but will not engage disaffected parents of youth who struggle with attendance. Offering attendance logs with grade entries at parent-teacher conferences are wonderful when the progress reports are wonderful, but if the reason for using such information is to help parents become accountable for youth who struggle, the results tend to produce angst and anger, not improved attendance.

Teaching

Solutions are not constructive when teachers perceive negative attitudes from their students and parents (e.g., teachers cannot fix lazy children nor make irresponsible parents accountable). Successful problem-to-solution building relies on using optimistic, teacher-controlled variables and characteristics. Table 10.7 lists some tentative problems and solutions that may help with school attendance issues.

Table 10.7. Teacher-Centered School Attendance Problems and Solutions

Problem	Solution	Remarks
Poor curricular relevance	Revise for relevance, accounting for background experiences while retaining rigor	Children who report to parents that they're bored in school or who spend large amounts of time in the nurse's office may be communicating disinterest
Teacher-driven parent-teacher conferences	Consider concrete strategies and tactics for creating collaborative settings; invite parent insights	Some parents are intimidated by school teachers and may not be forthcoming with concerns or ideas; others may feel judged; most will inform friends of perceptions of the school's reception of their children and themselves
Poor communications home	Consider alternatives to notes, email, phone calls at set times—determine parent availability and contact preferences, and plan accordingly	Notes and email are convenient for mass communications, but not necessarily effective; phone availability varies

Administration

Principals and other administrators are responsible, among other things, to keep children safe, keep teachers effectively teaching, and keep parents in the loop about any issues with their children. Working with children presents some special challenges, given the unique position of trust school staffs possess and the nature of helping vulnerable, immature children. While most principals and administrators are master teachers, deeply understanding teaching and learning processes, some find leadership roles incredibly demanding given the emotional nature that arrives with serving someone's child. Often, principals and other administrators, like teachers, turn toward comfortable schooling processes and practices to work through challenging circumstances, like how to communicate with upset parents about children who miss school or strained parent- and student-teacher relations. These meetings often take place at the principal or administrator's convenience at a school office that promotes school structure and authority, but, perhaps, not resolution. Sometimes, school officials seek ways of making sense of circumstances by reviewing and perpetuating self-serving history (e.g., the parents did not do well in school; we should expect no more from their children). Addressing attendance issues calls for different, more productive ways of thinking. Table 10.8 offers some provisional problems and solutions that may help with school attendance issues from an administrative standpoint.

Table 10.8. Administrative-Centered School Attendance Problems and Solutions

Problem	Solution	Remarks
Student health issues	Coordinate with support agencies for alternatives for health delivery, possibly using school facilities	Children with frequent or persistent health issues may need some basic medical assistance
Inflexible student rosters	Consider case managing students with propensities for absenteeism, recognizing staff strengths, and assign and reassign students accordingly	School youth may bond with different staff, respond to a new/different approach
One-size-fits-all discipline approach	Revise singular approaches with flexible responses focusing on student learning rather than consequences	Discipline varies across homes; some parents will side with their children if they do not share similar beliefs about common schooling discipline; consider integrating parental input

COMMUNITY-BASED PROBLEMS AND SOLUTIONS

It takes a village, not just school and family, to raise a child. Figuring out who dropped the ball and pointing fingers seem to be what politicians and many business and educational leaders do as we consider lists of schools and students who do well and do not do well by whatever measure. This cause-and-effect thinking is simplistic and seldom accurately identifies critical factors driving student success. While schools need to be places where children want to be, so should surrounding communities. Community and business leaders need to promote the importance of schooling, be involved in that schooling, and extend to children opportunities to learn in real-life circumstances. These experiences can be much more meaningful than some of the learning that takes place at a desk looking at a piece of paper covered with numbers. Table 10.9 offers some tentative problems and solutions that may be helpful. Time in school for youth is crucial for eventual school success. Constructively understanding why some children do not attend with regularity becomes important for consideration by school and community leadership.

Is attendance merely a result of parent or student choice? Are there impoverished urban and rural neighborhoods that are steep with barriers preventing school success? Are there cultural mores and norms that work in contentious ways with schools? If we simply pass and enforce laws to keep children in school, will this fix attendance? If we punish children for ditching by keeping them out of class and through suspension, does this really make sense? *Cause-and-effect thinking often misses critical points and core issues. Our assumptions and beliefs are often self-fulfilling and -perpetuating. How we frame issues skews our understanding of circumstance—we often jump from problems to solutions without clinical processes.*

Conventional response. Educators note a student misses a lot of school, seeks to visit the health office most days when in school, and has academic and social delays. Notes home do not come back to school. Phone messages go unanswered. Parents do not attend conferences. Administrative records indicate there have been problems with this child in the past. The teacher may pity the child's circumstances, categorize the child as "at-risk," reduce expectations, manage the relationship in "school-appropriate" ways, and dislike the unique challenges this child may present during classroom activities. The student says, "I hate the kids here," and seems to be disinterested more often than not. The principal may believe the teacher is very effective for "normal" students but negative about challenging youth, or get additional feedback from classified staff about

Table 10.9. Community-Centered School Attendance Problems and Solutions

Problem	Solution	Remarks
Lack of parent engagement/ leadership	Find ways (e.g., host dinners, honor parents) to target parents of children who struggle in schools, to initiate/sustain collaborative and volunteering opportunities, and to share decision-making across agencies	Parent participation is critical for student success in school
Misaligned values and mores	Find ways to capture insights from parents whose views differ from the norm; consider opportunities for improvement; engage community and business leaders for coherent approaches to helping parents/employees support children in school activities	Community and business leader investment in school processes can manifest through direct and indirect support (e.g., employers allowing needy parents time to transport youth to school)
Myths and rumors	Communicate in multiple ways (sending written notes to illiterate parents about the importance of writing is counterproductive); support and participate in community gatherings to address concerns, rumors	Employers and agency leaders should seek ways to help promote school activities and engage in related governance
Lack of community and business leader participation	Find ways to mentor youth who face barriers for success in school; support parents who face barriers with time and resources for helping ensure children are in school; participate in school governance	One-size-fits-all programs usually meet the needs of only a few students; committing time for needy youth yields higher returns than other resources
Schooling is an artificial process isolated from the community and other natural supports and resources	Find ways to integrate business, community, and school participation with service projects and internships that connect learning with doing	Curricular relevance and differentiation enrich learning experiences; getting community and business leader participation helps promote shared sense of schooling ownership
Mixed signals/ supports for impoverished and disenfranchised families	Find ways to consolidate service support agencies and resources under a single point of contact to help make systems rational and more economical; get school staff to consider issues from a family assets perspective	Parents and families with students who struggle with attendance often have needs that can be met by different constellations of service approaches

occasional misbehaviors on the bus, playground, and cafeteria. Community members may be concerned about this youth in stores and restaurants because attire and appearance suggest trouble. What do these assumptions and beliefs produce?

The teacher seeks to ensure one student does not diminish learning opportunities for other students and aggressively imposes classroom management practices. The teacher may file a special education or title services referral as needs exceed teaching capacity. The teacher and administrator may treat the parent(s) condescendingly because there is obviously a lack of support for helping the child succeed. Truancy laws may offer a basis for a call to law enforcement or protective services. Students who ditch often may benefit from significant amounts of time with disciplinary administrators offering policy-based, progressively punitive responses.

What are some possible assumptions and beliefs that drive such responses? *Our school process is perfectly rational. People have opportunities to make choices (and we all live in the same world so we must have the same choices). Some parents are not "good." Some youth are not "good." A child that misses school* benefits *from punishment. Telling others how to behave and think gets them in line, on track, and with the program.* These and similar thoughts do not usually yield productive outcomes. As indicated in the opening chapter, just as the "dropout problem" is not treatable in piecemeal fashion, neither is attendance "fixable" without productive concern for surrounding circumstances.

Systems Response

Action research methods using multiple sources and collection methods are more valid for clinically capturing and intervening in events then straight-line thinking. Assumptions or beliefs, rooted in optimism, tend to yield creative and productive frameworks. As context modulates circumstance, gaining key stakeholder input across critical school and community characteristics would help produce a picture that would be useful for pinpointing problem areas. Even as Charlotte Danielson's student achievement and Linda Lambert's leadership capacity for school improvement frameworks and rules of thumb are helpful for developing systems-perspective matrixes, school and community leadership should independently construct action research matrixes for adapting circumstances. Table 10.10, albeit abbreviated, offers an example of how to understand and engage a student who misses a lot of school.

Table 10.10. Action Research-Based Attendance Issues

Problem	Sources and Information	Remarks
Absenteeism – micro	Attendance records – Student missed 16 days, first semester	Student is struggling with school and showing some at-risk patterns
	Teacher observations – Student has social and academic delays, occasional discipline issues	Create strategies/tactics to gain parent input (e.g., home visit, work visit); address possible health concerns
	Staff observations – Student visits health office often, is occasionally mischievous	Create strategies/tactics to explore student reasoning (e.g., journal assignment exploring related themes), produce related curricula (e.g., assertive communications, socially appropriate behaviors)
	Parent concerns – Unknown	
	Student input – Disinterested in school, hates children in class	
Culture – macro	Parent surveys – School is productive, but does not invite parent participation in governance; some educators viewed as negative; overall relationship mixed	Create strategies/tactics to help all staff positively view and support "fringe" students
	Absenteeism rates – Student absenteeism rate is about 10% daily	Seek and act on parent and student reasoning for missing school
	Discipline process – Policy-driven, progressive	Use parent and student suggestions for creating discipline processes that are sensitive to circumstance
	Discipline data – High recidivism	Create meeting opportunities that are convenient to parents— at schools and elsewhere, at alternative times
	Parent-teacher conferences – At school, based on teacher convenience, centered on student performance and teacher expectations	Revise parent-teacher meetings to focus on student strengths and opportunities, seek collaboration; consider constructive ways to address performance issues (e.g., matching reading/entertainment preference with curricular approaches)

(Continued)

Table 10.10. Action Research-Based Attendance Issues (*Continued*)

Business roundtable focus group – Mixed collaboration between community leaders and the school; students are not usually prepared for workforce; teaching activities are largely school-housed; very little experiential, interactive learning occurs in communities; limited mentoring programs are "earned"	Access community resources and conduct experiential learning opportunities
	Engage community leaders to develop mentoring opportunities for all youth, but particularly those who need positive relationships

The Wilder Research Center, Amherst Wilder Foundation, synthesized research-based effective truancy prevention programs and have advanced the following effective practices:

- Relationship building: Students need individualized attention at school (this may explain why smaller schools have less absenteeism). Students need strong, positive relationships with teachers and other adults at school that are built on mutual trust and respect. In addition, research has found that older youth need strong and healthy relationships with peers and that these relationships can be a motivator for attending school.
- Contacting parents regarding absenteeism (works best with 10th grade and younger), creating meaningful incentives for parental responsibility, and including parents in all truancy prevention activities.
- Strong and clear attendance policies.
- Family counseling that recognizes and builds on the family's own strengths and resources, with the overall goal of increasing attendance (up to six months of family counseling, according to the study that found this approach effective).
- Intensive school interventions (examples include a mix of the above strategies and also mentors, individualized plans, a team approach, and "learning circles"). In learning circles, teachers provide education relevant to the cultural background of the community and provide a controlled environment that emphasizes academics and discipline.
- Establishing ongoing truancy prevention programs for school, rather than a onetime effort or an effort that only targets high-risk students.

- School staff members who are trained, committed, and supported to provide high-quality, responsive services and to keep at-risk youth in the educational mainstream.
- Ongoing, rigorous evaluation to measure the effect of the program with every approach taken.

Middle School

Adolescents hitting puberty make for exciting times, for both those youth and those who tend to those youth. Determining why these youth behave the way they do and for whatever reasons can be a rich experience dense with many challenges. These children often act on impulse and do things because they seem to be fun. Short-term planning is now, long-term planning is an hour from now. Peer pressure starts in earnest, school courses become markedly more difficult, and teachers seem more businesslike as schools appear more bureaucratic, less nurturing. And yet we have educators, parents, and other interested parties who see the behaviors and attitudes of these adolescents in straightforward ways, as if these youth know the same adult world, share the same adult experiences, and can make the same adult-informed choices.

Talk to those responsible for discipline of middle school children, be it at school, in the community, or at home, and we find there are usually significant challenges. We want kids to make good choices by punishing bad choices, but not by teaching alternatives. We look at those gangly youth as emergent adults with expectations that their thinking mirrors appearance. Yet we sometimes have middle school youth who are very immature or, in some cases, very mature. Both directions present special problems. We have adolescents with hormonal thoughts mixed with adolescents who are not there just yet, and we have bullying that can be terrifying for those who do not fit peer expectations. Academic achievement mirrors many of these problems.

For any who teach middle school adolescents core math, reading, and writing courses, the complications associated with mixed maturity levels are often compounded by mixed ability levels. Our politicians and leaders who have a simple, cause-and-effect understanding of human behavior and performance offer standardized expectations across subject areas in the hope that all children can meet those competencies. Really? How many successful business leaders cannot do algebra? We teach introduction to algebra in middle school, and for those who cannot understand why we use letters in math, this spells the beginning of how their challenges eventually emerge as beliefs of personal ineptitude. Should standardized levels of performance equal student performance, regardless of student readiness, teaching skills, and other systems-based factors?

What we tend to do with our challenging middle school students is make them retake the same class they failed because we assume they were simply making poor choices or being lazy, increase discipline (punishment) consequences for inappropriate behavior, and treat them as young adults with related reasoning skills. But are these approaches always useful or effective? No.

SCHOOL-BASED PROBLEMS AND SOLUTIONS

Exploring why middle school students misbehave can be a road to nowhere, yet there are great numbers of parents, educators, and community members who conceive of typical pre- and initial-pubescent behavior as a "choice" and consider youth who follow the rules as "good." The impulsive nature of middle school students, well known to any who serve this population, indicates controlling behavior can be similar to herding cats. Yet institutional schooling promotes great listings of what adolescents will not do and what will happen if they do. We have a host of discipline programs, intended to make discipline rationale and consistent, that usually work well for those so inclined to follow rules and focus through the many distractions (attractive peers, teachers, lunch menus, the game after school) that arrive with what many find as new responsibilities and freedoms. Get-tough, zero-tolerance rules mean we seek to punish, not to teach "discipline" (or, literally, to do the right thing without prompting). Teachers and others who struggle with meeting the needs of students who do not behave in mainstream ways tend to blame the students for disruption without introspection about how to promote a setting that is more accepting of different kinds of learners. Calls to parents can indicate more than "problem" adolescents. Such calls could indicate school staff incompetence or community member intolerance when working with these youth.

Compounding the impulsive behavior and mixed maturation we find in middle schools are youth at different academic readiness levels. Teachers and others commonly lament we should hold back those kids who are not ready for the next grade, assuming the child is making poor choices and without taking into account that adolescents interpret being held back as meaning they are "stupid" compared to peers. In either case, asking a child to repeat a grade without adapting instruction should offer anyone with a working definition of insanity pause—are we doing the same thing repeatedly and expecting different results? Getting tightly wrapped around standards and promoting rigorous instruction works if the instruction helps the student relate to content, allows the student to have authentic success, and is personally meaningful to the student. Teaching to the mainstream with paper-and-pencil methods passed on from generation to generation has yet to work for those who struggle (or even, in some cases, excel). Sending homework home to parents who work multiple jobs and may not be able to understand that work is not constructive. One-size-fits-all instructional methods convenient for teaching generally do not fit all children's needs.

Teaching

Solutions are not useful when teachers sense middle school students are "bad," are making poor choices, or are not academically ready. Getting problems-to-solutions right calls for educators to find positive, teacher-controlled issues. Table 10.11 lists some problem and solution suggestions that may help with middle school issues.

Table 10.11. Teacher-Centered Middle School Problems and Solutions

Problem	Solution	Remarks
Poor curricular relevance	Revise for relevance, accounting for background experiences, while retaining rigor	Sitting still in seats doing paperwork for 60 minutes is not constructive for most students; adolescents can learn playing games or using other engaging methods; properly managed group work can teach content and collaboration skills
Teacher-driven parent-teacher conferences	Consider concrete strategies and tactics for creating collaborative settings that invite parental insights	Some parents can't do the middle school homework; some feel pressure to conform or advocate for their children "against" the school; getting parent enfranchisement into school practices could be critical for helping youth who struggle
Poor communications home	Consider alternatives to notes, email, phone calls at set times—determine parent availability and contact preferences, and plan accordingly	Parents need to hear about student success, not just problems; communicating unconditional regard for wishes for student success can promote positive teacher-parent relations more than singular focus on detailing deficits

Administration

Middle school administration engages the special challenges that arrive with pre- and newly pubescent youth. Typically wonderful teachers, these administrators seek to keep children safe, teachers proficient, parents informed, community involved, and a host of bureaucrats happy with reports. Discipline and academic progress are particularly challenging issues given the emotional and political nature that arrives with such deliberations.

Is discipline a no-nonsense crime-and-punishment process? Do some parents want to know that if their kid gets three days' worth of lunch detention for tossing food in the cafeteria, everyone else that did the same gets the same? Do some parents seek mercy? Do some parents want school officials to use the paddle? From an educator's perspective, meeting the wide-ranging expectations from different homes and a community can be daunting and not possible. If a kid ditches school, should we then suspend that kid to teach a lesson? Really?

What about the child who struggles in the math class and reports the teacher is mean? Do administrators dictate, in mature terms, the appropriate response to this circumstance by holding only the adolescent accountable? Do administrators protect teachers? Should they? When educators talk about a child failing a course, is the focus only on what the child is doing or not doing, or, in even more unconstructive ways, on how the parents are not holding their children accountable? Is the schooling system the "answer" and any who do not succeed the "problem"? Addressing middle school issues calls for different, helpful ways of thinking. Table 10.12 offers some tentative problems and solutions that may help with middle school issues from administrative standpoints.

COMMUNITY-BASED PROBLEMS AND SOLUTIONS

Do community and business leaders embrace or shy away from adolescents? Do we need to hire staff to monitor kids to prevent theft or property damage? As teens develop their own voices and immature understandings of their surroundings, do the adults engage or dispute these notions of reality? Do adults push for kids to think, but the moment they do, ask them to be quiet so as not to show ignorance? Do we avoid supervising adolescents and then lament what unsupervised adolescents do? In short, do our communities and businesses welcome adolescents in developmentally appropriate ways (e.g., ample supervision before and after school, opportunities to participate in healthy and appropriate physical activities, job shadowing, mentoring)?

Middle school years are tough. They are tough for adolescents and those who care about those adolescents. How business and community leaders

Table 10.12. Administrative-Centered Middle School Problems and Solutions

Problem	Solution	Remarks
Students failing core math, reading, and writing courses	Supervise instruction predicated on student and not teacher performance; facilitate creative teaching approaches that cross learning modalities and interests	Adapting instruction to needs instead of using remedial courses increases chances of authentic student success
Bullying	Keep staff in problem areas (e.g., playground, lunchroom, hallways); promote positive relations between staff and students; find ways to get youth who struggle with authority into leadership roles	Teachers and staff (including principals) should seek non-class times to build relations with students; educators should model respectful behavior (no sarcasm or embarrassment aimed at kids)
One-size-fits-all discipline approach	Revise singular approaches with flexible responses focusing on student learning more than on consequences; integrate parent and student collaboration	Discipline focused on learning instead of punishing, cued to students, bodes well for increased chances of changing dispositions and behaviors; following the same one-size-fits-all approaches doesn't usually change student behavior because most middle and high school principals work with the same "problem" groups in any given school year
Participation in extracurricular activities are based on merit	Helping youth connect to strong role models in schools increases chances youth may persevere through difficult courses or other challenges	Offering children opportunities to shine in their strengths bodes well for increased chances of overall schooling success

engage these self-absorbed youth has significant long-term implications. If systems thinking is more about how many factors affect a young teen and less about how some teacher or parent or school staff member is responsible for what a youth does, the community looms large in the education of its resident youth.

Table 10.13. Community-Centered Middle School Problems and Solutions

Problem	Solution	Remarks
Lack of parental engagement and leadership	Initiate and support parent and youth groups; promote healthy parenting; find ways to celebrate exceptional parenting success	Most parents want their kids to do well—how this happens varies just as parenting approaches vary; traditional judgment tends to divide rather than unify
Misaligned values and mores	Community, business, and school leaders should work collaboratively toward producing consistent and caring approaches for helping youth who struggle in academics and social behavior; a collective vision with objectives may help shift the adult response from being punitive toward disciplining with regard	Kids are more likely to change disposition and behavior in response to someone who cares and rewards positive behavior than to fear of punishment
Schooling is an artificial process, isolated from the community with its natural supports and resources	Find ways to integrate business, community, and school participation with service projects and internships that connect learning with doing	Youth need to gain an authentic sense of success because most people avoid what they do not do well—extending opportunities in natural, real-world ways may help students connect relevance and be successful

So, is behavior just a choice, especially bad behavior? Do community and business leaders judge youthful indiscretions in the same ways we judge adults? While there should certainly be consequences for behavior as a means to help with learning, is the focus punishment? Should it be? Do community and business leaders shun "problem" youth? How do community and business leaders engage those kids who struggle with being socially appropriate? Do we tend to find the problems we look for, given that problem children are, after all, problem children? Are there schooling implications?

Many of our youth who struggle with behavior also struggle with school, particularly courses that can become very demanding when those kids do not understand the content and its relevance. As students learn how to diagram sentences or use new abstract concepts to manipulate numbers, they may have parents who are lost in these processes. Student success may only center on what is found in communities. Student confidence in risk taking could be shaped by how community and business leaders interact and by how failure is embraced (e.g., punishment or discipline orientation).

Conventional Response

Educators note a student has "attitude," struggles with math and reading, and bullies peers on the playground. Calls home yield upset parents who indicate to teachers that their child was not raised to misbehave. Parent-teacher conferences focus on poor performance and bad behavior, with teacher admonishments about being consistent in discipline and helping with homework. Nothing changes. The teachers begin to dampen expectations and look for ways to get this child out of the room, given the distractions and inconvenience. The student hates school and most kids at the school. The student knows the assistant principal well through routine visits. This adolescent gets adult company as he or she walks around in stores because he or she is not trusted. No mentoring organization reaches out to help. The police recognize this child as trouble, given non-conformist dress and mannerisms. The principal has labeled this kid a chip off the old block, knowing that his or her dad or mom was a handful back in the day. Remedial courses are offered, but the child chooses not to help self. Parents blame the school as an uncaring institution, the same kind they attended. All the parents hear is about how their child is a poor excuse for a human being, suggesting the parents do not know how to parent. The child is held back a grade, resents being retained, and does not think doing the same thing again and again is helpful.

What are some possible reasons that drive this sad circumstance? *Schools and communities make perfect sense. They are without flaw. Kids need to adapt to what adults want, regardless of ability or experience. Kids who look like adults think like adults. Everyone shares the same set of values, or should.* These simplistic, cause-and-effect assumptions have yet to produce desirable results for kids who struggle in social and academic settings.

Systems Response

Action research could help this situation by using different sources and methods for understanding and intervening rather than using straight-line thinking resulting in unintended outcomes. Optimism and ownership of the "problem" is critical as part of the first step because we can change systems and frames of references much easier than changing that difficult adolescent.

John Guthrie and Marcia Davis offer six steps to help motivate middle school students who struggle with reading:

1. Construct rich knowledge goals as the basis of instruction
2. Use real-world interactions to connect instruction to student experiences
3. Afford students an abundance of interesting curricular materials
4. Provide some choice among material to engage
5. Give direct instruction for important learning strategies
6. Encourage collaboration in many aspects of learning [adapted from J. T. Guthrie and M. H. Davis (2003), "Motivating struggling readers in middle school through engagement model of classroom practice," *Reading & Writing Quarterly*, 19(1), 59–85. © Taylor & Francis Ltd, http//www .infomaworld.com, reprinted by permission of the publisher.]

Table 10.14. Action Research-Based Middle School Issues

Problem	Sources and Information	Remarks
Performance and behavior – micro	Student struggles with basic literacy competencies as indicated by pretest	Student is missing critical sub-elements for understanding instruction; accommodations in pace, content, and relevance are needed to promote authentic success
	Teacher observations – Student has social and academic delays, discipline issues	Explicit and respectful discussions about school expectations are needed; student and parent input should be sought on how to help move toward related goals (instead of focusing on punitive measures and in anticipation of gradual success)
	Staff observations – Student is teased on playground and on bus, is occasionally mischievous	Find ways to communicate authentic regard for the student separate from academic and social successes
	Parent concerns – Uncaring school staff, child is a target singled out for punishment, embarrassed because of difficulties with core subjects	Create strategies/tactics to explore student reasoning (e.g., journal assignment exploring related themes), produce related curricula (e.g., assertive communications, socially appropriate behaviors)
	Student input – Hates teachers, most peers; doesn't feel like help is available	

(Continued)

Table 10.14. Action Research-Based Middle School Issues (*Continued*)

Culture – macro	Parent surveys – School is traditional and expectations are clear; some students are pegged as favorites, others as trouble; some teachers are viewed as mean, uncaring	Create strategies/tactics to help all staff positively view and support "fringe" students
	Discipline data – About 5% of the student population spends about 50% of their school time in the principal's office for disciplinary action	Seek and act on parent and student reasoning for conduct in school
	Discipline process – Policy-driven, educator-driven	Integrate parent and student suggestions for creating discipline processes that are sensitive to circumstance
	Parent-teacher conferences – At school, based on teacher convenience, centered on student performance and behavior, and teacher expectations	Create meeting opportunities that are convenient to parents—at schools and elsewhere, at alternative times
	Business raundtable focus group – Mixed collaboration between community leaders and the school; students are not usually prepared for workforce; teaching activities are largely school-housed; very little experiential, interactive learning occurs in communities; limited mentoring programs are "earned"	Revise parent-teacher meetings to focus on student strengths and opportunities, seek collaboration; consider constructive ways to address performance issues (e.g., matching reading/entertainment preference with curricular approaches)
		Access community resources and conduct experiential learning
		Engage community leaders to develop mentoring opportunities for all youth, but particularly those who need positive relationship opportunities

Core Courses

The high school youth who struggle the most with English, math, and other core courses take the most English, math, and other core courses—over and over and over. As school staffs face mounting and increasing pressures for helping all youth achieve at high levels of math, English, and other core course performance, those students who struggle in these critical areas are being left further and further behind, given the fast pace, content that doesn't help with gaps, and often singular ways of instruction that are not relevant to the youth's world. Many of these students would rather drop out of school than go to the same class for the same instruction to prove, yet again, how stupid they are in English, math, and other core courses.

When we talk to those responsible for teaching high school youth who struggle with core concepts, we often hear teachers, parents, and others lament about how these teens make poor choices and are lazy. Sometimes we hear of poor home or community lives, no homework being done, poor parenting and teaching, negative school culture—the list goes on and on. The ready-made answer for the teen who fails world history is to take world history again without consideration, from the student's perspective, of why the student failed world history. Is the material interesting? Does learning happen separately from just writing thoughts on paper? Is any of the history connected to what is going on today, in the teen's world? All this finger-pointing and scapegoating and taking courses over and over and over has yet to lead toward positive outcomes for students who struggle with math, English, and other core courses.

SCHOOL-BASED PROBLEMS AND SOLUTIONS

Effectively exploring why some youth struggle with math, English, and other core courses should not include placing blame on the student who struggles, but parents, educators, and others tend to do just this—blame the student for inadequacies based on poor choices rooted in poor attitudes. Are schooling and home teaching practices perfect? Do teens learn differently? Do adults learn differently? Do we teach only by methods in which we find comfort? Could the mindset of the teacher who considers himself or herself a "math teacher," not a teacher of children, suggest that content is central in teaching—where is the teen in this notion, especially that teen who struggles?

Offering dumbed-down remedial courses for the none-too-bright group (ability grouping) is convenient for teachers but not supportive for student learning. Many educators struggle when trying to reach across the broad range of skills and readiness levels in the thirty or so youth who populate a given room taking a particular course. Could fun, engaging, multisensory, and rigorous instruction possibly be more productive in this setting instead of asking youth to get out paper and pencil and answer questions 1–20 out of some book? Is school a "hoop" to be jumped through? Should it be?

Teaching

Any teacher who thinks some teen is making poor choices and has a bad attitude has a built-in excuse for non-performance—blame the kid and the teacher has no accountability for how he or she is part of this teen's orbit. Getting the problem centered constructively means using optimism and considering what the teacher can control. Table 10.15 lists some problem and solution suggestions that may help with core course issues.

Administration

A big challenge for school leadership is to find ways to support teachers and hold them accountable for developing teaching knowledge, skills, and abilities. Another big challenge is to find optimistic ways to meet the concerns of parents who may not share the same values and perceive that the school staff lacks regard or skill for helping the struggling teen. Another big challenge is how to engage the community in schooling. Through it all, administration needs to establish personal, caring relations with the students—especially those who struggle.

Table 10.15. Teacher-Centered School Core Course Problems and Solutions

Problem	Solution	Remarks
Content-centered instruction	Revise for relevance, accounting for background experiences while retaining rigor	Curricular content should minimally mirror cultural composition of student body, and account for community and regional activities
Ability grouping, remedial courses	Leverage group and community activities with mixed ability groups to promote learning in multisensory ways; promote team learning and authentic opportunities for student success	Students feel "stupid" when put in with "stupid" courses and groups—learning potential is diminished in such settings
Marked up papers, critical comments	Feedback centered on strengths with opportunities instead of deficits suggest authentic potential	Negative marks and comments are punitive and research shows they do not help struggling learners "get it"—rather, such commentary further substantiates notions of ineptitude

Table 10.16. Administrative-Centered School Core Course Problems and Solutions

Problem	Solution	Remarks
Students failing math, English, and other core courses	Facilitate clinical assessment of teaching methods, offer suggestions to help with instructional processes to meet gaps in student learning	Find ways to help the student sense relevance and have authentic success; could the shop teacher help with basics in grammar or algebraic concepts during a favorite activity?
One-size-fits-all remedial approach	Adapt learning plans to help with individual students; facilitate targeted assistance	Student sense of self-competence and subsequent learning are affected by placement; doing the same thing over and over usually produces boredom, not learning

Do administrators link professional development and student performance in teacher evaluations? Are teachers aware of where they stand in terms of discipline issue rates or referrals for special services compared with peers? Are student and parent comments about teacher attitudes integrated into performance evaluations? Should administration retain school staff who are largely viewed as mean to students and parents? Do administrators excuse teachers of tough subjects for resulting high rates of student failure with the rationale that the course is rigorous? Do administrators protect teachers against angry parents frustrated with poor student performance or against frustrated students who feel disrespected? How involved should administration be in promoting energetic, engaging, and rigorous instruction, or is this in the teacher's domain? Is the status quo working? How would administration know? Table 10.16 lists some problem and solution suggestions that may help with core course issues.

COMMUNITY-BASED PROBLEMS AND SOLUTIONS

Should community members help schooling by sanctioning those students who do not do well in school? Should, for example, work opportunities be linked to school grades? Should community leaders engage in identifying poor school and teacher performance to help weed out those educators who are harming instead of helping our youth learn and grow? Do community members and leaders conceive of school as *the only place* where students learn?

Table 10.17. Community-Centered School Core Course Problems and Solutions

Problem	Solution	Remarks
Lack of access for mentoring	Community, business, and school leaders should look to identify mentoring groups that attract youth who struggle with core academics	Facilitate variety of youth-service organizations that offer those who struggle in school opportunities for learning in constructive ways; avoid merit-based entry and participation, as this reduces entry chances for those who most need the mentoring services
Lack of internship and job shadowing opportunities	Community, business, and school leaders should work collaboratively with school staff to offer students real-world opportunities to connect value of core courses with job opportunities	Learning authentic applications in real-world settings improves chances that youth will understand why working hard to master difficult concepts might have personal benefit

What role does the community assume in helping youth who struggle with math, English, and other core courses? Table 10.17 offers some community-based suggestions for helping students who struggle with core courses.

Some people, youth and adults, struggle with math, English, or other core courses largely because of lack of relevance. Some struggle because of poor relations with the teacher who taught that subject. Some struggle because other life events were overwhelming when engaged in some course. Some struggle because reading is a chore, listening to endless lecturing is a chore, or the "helpful" curriculum is not helpful. Some struggle because their developmental stage does not match school-structured assembly-line notions of what should be known by what age. Some struggle because teachers teach at a pace that works well with assembly-line notions of learning production. Some struggle because of poor instruction.

Teens find value and self-worth in how they measure up, or down, compared to their newly emerging, incredibly influential peers. Those who have struggled with math since 5th grade, who have "benefited" from extra homework and remedial classes that offer the same material in the same way, repeatedly, are or become firmly convinced of their ineptitude—hardly a helpful attitude for driving the kind of energy needed to help understand incomprehensible concepts.

Conventional Response

Given the failing grade in the 9th grade pre-algebra course, educators note that a sophomore has not yet mastered basic algebraic concepts. The parents indicate they also struggled with high school math. The student appears indifferent about having to take the course again, now with mostly freshmen. No one seems interested enough to consult the student's academic records to see that standardized tests since 5th grade in math and other core areas suggest the student struggles mightily with abstract and reading concepts. This youth excels in music, but he or she is ineligible to participate in after-school programs because of the poor performance in math and other core literacy courses. With the newfound free time, this teen recently got a job in the community bussing tables. Management appreciates the youth's strong work ethic. Parents do not seek nor do they receive positive information about what their child does in school. The only contacts are based on how the child is making poor choices by not turning in homework or not completing all assignments in math and English classes. The teen has indicated to teachers and parents that the courses are hard. Despite the teen's best efforts, teachers seem to think the issue is student laziness. The teen does not understand most of the instructions and does not feel respected enough by the teachers or finds the schooling process too hard to ask for help. The teen finds himself or herself in the same place that his or her parents did in school—dealing with uncaring teachers and struggling through irrelevant courses.

How did we get here? Do educators, community leaders, and even youth consider challenges in making learning work the sole responsibility of the teen who struggles? How does the framing, attribution, or fault of responsible adults possibly contribute to the issue? Could the problem be how people *see* the problem?

Systems Response

Comprehensive, balanced research could help this situation by tapping into different sources and methods for trying to see the whole picture instead of convenient portions of the picture. As indicated earlier, having an optimistic problem owned by those taking action would be the initial step needed for effecting change.

Amy Azzam offers a list of dropout prevention steps distilled from research targeting the reasoning of those who left school:

1. Make school more engaging through real-world, experiential learning
2. Provide improved instruction and supports for struggling learners
3. Improve school climate

Table 10.18. Action Research-Based Core Course Issues

Problem	Sources and Information	Remarks
Performance and behavior – micro	Student struggles with critical core concepts	Student is missing critical sub-elements needed to understand instruction; accommodations in pace, content, and relevance are needed to promote authentic success
	Teacher observations – Student appears disinterested and disengaged in math and English courses	Participation in school activities could offer important relationship with educators, authentic success; linking performance with courses and unrelated extracurricular activities is rational for schools, not necessarily for students
	Staff observations – Student does well in shop classes, fits in well with friends; has untapped musical talent	Educators need to find ways to communicate to parents authentic regard for the student separate from academic and social successes, and seek parents' and students' input on how to make school coursework relevant and ways to increase chances of academic success
	Parent concerns – Uncaring school staff, child doesn't get needed help	
	Student input – Disinterested in math and English, doesn't relate with anyone on staff, thinks most school classes are boring and non-useful	
Culture – macro	Parent surveys – School is viewed as helpful for many, some parents and administrators show favoritism, not all children are treated equally, schoolwork is paper- and book-based	Create strategies/tactics to help all staff members positively view and support "fringe" students

(Continued)

Table 10.18. Action Research-Based Core Course Issues (*Continued*)

Problem	Sources and Information	Remarks
	Remediation process – Policy-driven, educator-driven	Seek and act on standardized test data, and parent and student reasoning for adapting instruction
	Parent-teacher conferences – At school, based on teacher's convenience, centered on student performance and behavior, and teacher's expectations	Seek alternatives to having youth who fail courses retake the same courses
	Business roundtable focus group – Poor collaboration between community leaders and the school, students are not usually prepared for workforce, teaching activities are largely school-housed, very little experiential, interactive learning occurs in communities, mentoring activities are "earned"	Revise parent-teacher meetings to focus on student strengths and opportunities, seek collaboration; consider constructive ways to address performance issues (e.g., matching reading/ entertainment preference with curricular approaches)
		Access community resources and conduct experiential learning opportunities
		Engage community leaders to develop mentoring opportunities for all youth, but particularly those who need positive relationships

4. Ensure that students have a relationship with at least one adult in the school
5. Improve communication between parents and schools [adapted from Amy Azzam, "Special Report: Why Students Drop Out," *Educational Leadership*, 64(7), 91–93. © 2007 by ASCD. Reprinted with permission. Learn more about ASCD at www.ascd.org.]

STANDARDIZED VS. CLASSROOM PERFORMANCE

Perhaps the most difficult and important problem found in the dropout study involved the *owls and turtles* finding. In short, the youth who did really well on standardized measures in core reading, math, and English tests did consistently better in classroom performance based on grades. These are the *owls*. Unfortunately, those who did not do well on standardized measures in core reading, math, and English tests did ever-more poorly in classroom performance based on grades. These are the *turtles*. What emerges is how vitally important perceptions of youth schooling ability (or inability) seem to affect teachers', parents', and other interested community members' expectations. Do we teach down to the slow kids or up to the fast kids? Do we anticipate that our troubled teen is trouble because his or her parents were trouble, his or her siblings were trouble, the cultural background is trouble, the last teacher said this youth was trouble, or the way that the youth dresses is trouble? Could the child's culture not work in complete harmony with the caring adult's culture? Could there be some judgment going on here?

Oftentimes, teachers, parents, and community leaders seek tactics and techniques to help resolve problems. Perhaps how we address the problem is not about *what we do*, but *why we do what we do*. Are those youth who struggle in school settings viewed as trouble, extra work for the caring adult, a drag on energy and attention, defiant, or delinquent? How do we fix any of this? *Can* we fix any of this?

Could that same youth be seen as a challenge, a blessing to help professionals extend practice, parents to extend patience, and community members to extend ways to capture a sense of community engaging those who struggle with traditional schooling? Are schooling practices perfectly rational and above reproach? Are parents perfect? Are communities perfect?

The basis for systems thinking and ecological systems should move us past simply knowing problems to deeply seeking problems-turned-to-solutions in constructive ways. We know the system is complex. We know there are no easy, one-size-fits-all answers. We know naysayers and realists, lost in their own notions of negative truths without benefit of reflection, lead us to angst and the perpetuation of problems. The notion that some kids are very smart and some are not can be a very damning assumption for those who are not in the in-group.

How do we know what our beliefs are? Why do we push one child but not the other? Do we resent or fear the child who does not share in our view of truth? Can we show deep respect and love for all children, even those we struggle with? Should we?

Epilogue

What started out as two seemingly simple research questions grew into a landmark longitudinal study and eventually the book you have just read. In the beginning stages of this study our intent was not to publish a "stand-alone" book of this nature. Rather, as researchers, we were simply curious as to whether one could pinpoint along the developmental pathway where problems surfaced and began to go wrong for those children who would eventually drop out of school. When we discovered that dropouts were different than graduates as early as kindergarten in all educational, family, and behavior variables, we were somewhat surprised. So surprised, in fact, that we had to go back and check the data to be sure what we found were indeed the correct findings. Sadly, the data were correct. It was at this point our thoughts shifted toward the creation of a book that could help parents, educators, and community stakeholders identify key points of interventions for such wayward youth.

Yes, children do drop out of school in kindergarten. Even more alarming is that preventing and finding a solution for this developmental outcome has remained elusive to parents, educators, community stakeholders, and governmental officials for over a century. Why? Because dropping out of school is not conceptualized or considered an issue that originates, develops, persists, and comes to fruition at the elementary level of education. Rather, we conceptualize high school dropouts as an issue that originates, develops, and comes to fruition at the high school or secondary level of education. Indeed, don't we call them *high school* dropouts? Given that our study clearly demonstrates that high school dropouts drop out of school long before high school, we believe examining this issue from a systems approach be considered near the forefront of our nation's educational agenda during the elementary level of education, long before a child enters high school.

Knowing that each level of education at each successive grade builds upon earlier and prior levels of education in the educational framework, the question becomes, why don't parents, educators, community stakeholders, and governmental officials focus their efforts on addressing the dropout phenomena at the elementary level of education? The answer to that is based on three inherent flaws of the education system and American society in general—namely, results, speed, and standardization.

Our education system is housed in a society that demands results—*now*. Further, we live in a society that is far more interested in and gravitates toward results as opposed to understanding actual problems. Focusing our efforts at the elementary level does not provide educators the immediate results they are looking for—they have to wait several years for the outcomes to come to fruition. If understanding the problem doesn't help parents and educators come up with a quick fix to help children get through school in the "here and now," it's not worth the effort.

We live in a society where political, community, and educational leaders need quick results to help shape their campaign agendas and bolster their chances of being reelected. Studying dropouts at the elementary level does not support their educational platforms of "results now." In addition, we live in a society that is driven by the media. The media is not interested in understanding phenomena or problems. Rather, the media is interested in solutions, quick fixes, or a "good story." In fact, the media has a better story when the dropout rate increases and students are not graduating high school because they failed the state exit exams. That story will make the front page of the news. Think it won't? It did in Arizona on August 25, 2005. Rather than ask educators and researchers how to address the problem, the article predicted doomsday for Arizona without understanding the problem at hand.

The name of the game is speed. Why the need for speed? Because our education system, like our society, operates in fire drill mode and demands answers instantly, spontaneously, pronto, rapido, stat, now, and yesterday. With the advancement of technology, our patience grows thinner while our demands grow exponentially. The more important a societal issue, the more we seek instant results. However, when it comes to understanding a problem such as dropouts, speed kills.

Teachers are expected to conform and respond to school policies, principals are expected to conform to district policies, district superintendents are expected to conform to county policies, and so on, up to the national level. From the national level down to the teacher in the child's classroom, results must comply with standards and everyone must produce results yesterday.

We live in a society where schools can be taken over by the state if results are not produced within a couple of years. Following children from kindergarten through graduation or to the point of dropping out of school does not fit into the mold of speed, spontaneous results, and instant feedback used by our education system and our society.

When it comes to education, the three rules of engagement are standardization, standardization, and standardization. Why? We live in a bureaucratic society that is so layered from the national government to the state departments of education, to the county superintendents, to the district superintendents, to the school principals, to the teachers, to the parents, and finally to the children themselves that we have created an education system of continual paper trails that handcuff and prevent parents and local educators from making a move without being scrutinized or placed in some level of accountability. Chants and cries of "standardization," "unification," "aligning," "streamlining," and the creation of "common" curricula, textbooks, and teaching methods have created an educational system that has paralyzed the imagination and creativity of children, stripped away any notion of individuality among children, and ultimately overlooked the human ecology of life. Basically, the education system we have today suffers from paralysis by analysis. Or said differently, the education system suffers from *insamity*—that is, the pathological need to create sameness.

The problem with such a method of thinking and operating is that there is no such thing as a "standardized" child, a "unified" child, a "common" child, or an "aligned" child. Children develop differently and have multiple systems in their lives that affect development. This presents a problem because the current view of our educational system, from national government to local schools, focuses on "standardization," "unification," "commonalities," "aligning," and other nice ideas of putting everyone into the same petri dish.

If our society is truly interested in understanding the dropout phenomenon, then we need parents, educational leaders, business leaders, community leaders, and political leaders to look beyond quick fixes, a good story, and standardizing our children and educational system. We need to step away from the current practice of believing children drop out of school because they had bad teachers or we need to hire excellent teachers or we need to bring them up to speed or they need core classes or they need before- or after-school classes. That is not why children drop out of school. This institutionally centered, flawed belief that children develop in an educational vacuum is held by countless educators and it prevents them from coming to grips with this problem of children dropping out of school. Period.

If educators could borrow the training of researchers grounded in educational psychology, they could help parents and educational, business, community, and political leaders understand that you have to identify a problem before you can begin to address the purpose of your study or actions. You cannot produce reliable findings or results from a study unless you have a solid research design. You cannot generate strategies to keep children in school until you have a reason to do so. You cannot know what the reasoning for generating strategies is unless you understand the problem at hand.

We need to move beyond simple cause-and-effect thinking and toward understanding the problem of why children drop out of school. Unless we begin to examine the human ecology of children and address the multiple layers or systems that operate daily on children, we will not get the results we are looking for. Yes, we will get results. But did we get the results based on identifying the problem? Or did we get the results because we rushed and wanted quick fixes at the high school level rather than taking our time to truly understand the problem and focus across the developmental pathway and human ecology of children? Did we look for the lazy child and believe we found the lazy child (when, in fact, we are lazy in how we come to know what our problem may be, and how we need to include ourselves when trying to sort out the problem)?

Although this study was retrospective in nature, it still followed the developmental pathways of graduates and dropouts from four separate cohorts from the beginnings of their school careers in kindergarten to the end points of either graduation or dropping out of high school. Much can be gained from this study if we are willing to take the time to understand the problem of why kids drop out of school. We must move toward examining the human ecology of children as opposed to simply focusing on educational variables; we must change our priorities from demanding results, speed, and standardization to really focusing on children as humans and understanding their developmental pathways. In other words, it's time for parents, teachers, business leaders, community leaders, and political leaders to place real meaning behind the idea of "No Child Left Behind."

Index

Guthrie, John, 100

Head Start, 15
Hickman, Greg, 3
high school, ix–x, 1–2, 4–5, 7–9, 11,
  16–20, 21, 22–23, 26–32, 36–37, 39,
  41, 43, 45, 46, 55–56, 58–60, 67–68,
  71, 76, 84, 101–2, 105, 106, 111–12,
  114
Hispanic, 7, 13, 18
homework, *76*, 77, 95, 102, 105, 106
human ecology, x, 1, 20, 46, 60, 65,
  71–109, 113

impulsive, 93, 94
institutional thinking/processes, 2, 59,
  81–82, 84, 94, 113
intellectual quotient (IQ), 61, *62*

job shadowing, 96, *105*
juvenile court/juvenile justice, 5, 8, 10,
  18–19, *59. See also* discipline

kindergarten, x, 1–3, 4, 8, 10, 11, 18,
  21–22, 37, 39–40, 45, 51–53, 55, 56,
  60, 67–68, 71, 80–81, *82, 83*, 84, *85*,
  111, 113, 114

Lambert, Linda, 90
language, 3, 5, 10, 18, 30–31, *34*
laziness/lazy, 57, 68, 81, 86, 94, 102,
  106, 114
literacy, 2–3, 15, 60, 81, 83–84, *100*, 106
Locke, John, 37
"locus of control," 75
low family income, 5, 14–15, 53
low socioeconomic status (SES), 5, 14

macrosystem, 72–73, *73*
mathematics, 8, 9, 10, 22, 23, *24*, 27,
  28–29, *31, 32, 33*, 46, *47*, 49, 50, 51,
  52, 53, 62–64, 68, 93, 96, *97*, 101–2,
  104, 105, 106, 109

mentoring programs, 3, 74, *92, 101*
mesosystem, 72, *73*
microsystem, 72–73, *73*
middle-class values, 81
middle school, x, 3, 8, 47–53, 55, 80,
  93–94, 95–97, 100
mobility, 5, *15*, 17, 18, 20, 53, 74
motivation, 75, 92, 100
music, 18, 22

National Center for Children in Poverty,
  42
National Curve Equivalency (NCE), 10,
  29–32, *33–35*, 36
National Dropout Prevention Center,
  42
Native American, 7, 13
negative attitudes/experiences, 42, 53,
  80, 82, 86, 102
No Child Left Behind (NCLB), ix, 7,
  58, 73, 74, 114
norms, 72, 73, 74, 88

older siblings, 5, *15*, 16–17
one-size-fits-all approaches, 42, 55–56,
  68, *82, 85, 87, 89*, 95, *97, 104*, 109
"on track," 46, 52–53, 57, 58–60,
  67–68, 71, 90
optimism/optimistic, 79, 80, 82, 86, 90,
  99, 103, 106
owls and turtles, 109

parents, ix, x, 8, 10, 16, 39, 53, 56, 59,
  60, 61, 64, 68, 69, 71, 72, 73, 77,
  79, 80–81, *82, 83, 85*, 87, 92, 94, 96,
  102, 104, 106, 109, 111, 112, 113;
  engagement/involvement, 42, *89, 98,
  100–101, 107*; neglect, 80; parent-
  teacher conferences, 61, *86*, 88, *91,
  95, 99, 101, 108*; poor, 4–5
Patterson, Gerald, 4
peer pressure, 93
physical education, 9, 22

tabula rasa, 37
teachers. *See* educators
Title I services, 10, 15, 20, 53
total quality management (TQM), 74
transcripts, 8–9
truancy prevention, 92–93
t-test, 45

"usual suspects," 1–5, 15–16, 18, 20, 53, 64, 71

vocabulary, 10, 31, *35*
vocational courses, 17, 20

Western Interstate Commission for Higher Education, 5
Wilder Research Center, Amherst Wilder Foundation, 92
writing, 8, 22, 23, *24*, 84, 93

Z scores, 62

About the Authors

Gregory P. Hickman, Ph.D., moved to Arizona in 2004 to become the director of the Arizona Dropout Initiative. His research has primarily focused on adolescent problem behaviors. More specifically, how does parenting impact such adolescent behavior? In addition, his research has focused on programmatic evaluation including evaluating adolescent programs for Procter & Gamble, Maricopa Community Colleges. He lives with his wife Tammy, two boys Alex and Zach, and three labs (Woody, Cooper, and Earle—yes, all named after Ohio State football coaches).

Randy S. Heinrich, D.M., served for over a decade as an educator in a rural Arizona school district, with research interests in dropout prevention and alternative schools. While he currently serves as faculty for Argosy University Online, Randy, his bride Donna, and their dogs reside in the beautiful White Mountains of Arizona.

CPSIA information can be obtained at www.ICGtesting.com
Printed in the USA
BVOW010408201011

274096BV00002B/5/P